SECOND-HAND
SHOCK

ALSO BY ELLIE IZZO AND VICKI CARPEL MILLER

Just Stop Doing That
Just Stop Picking Losers
Just Stop Eating That

ALSO BY ELLIE IZZO

The Bridge To I Am

SECOND-HAND SHOCK
Surviving & Overcoming Vicarious Trauma

Ellie Izzo, PhD, LPC
and
Vicki Carpel Miller, BSN, MS, LMFT

High Conflict Institute Press
High Conflict Institute, LLC
Scottsdale, Arizona

Published by: HCI Press, A Division of High Conflict Institute, LLC
7701 E. Indian School Rd., Ste. F, Scottsdale, AZ 85251, (602) 606-7628, (888) 768-9874
www.hcipress.com

Library of Congress Control Number: 2010942619

ISBN-10: 1-936268-21-3
ISBN-13: 978-1-936268-21-4

Publisher:
Published by High Conflict Institute Press
www.hcipress.com

PRESS Printed in the United States of America

This book is dedicated
to all of our clients –
past, present and future.

CONTENTS

ABOUT THE AUTHORS

Ellie Izzo, PhD, LPC

Ellie Izzo has been in clinical practice for over 30 years. She also serves as a trainer, Divorce Coach and Child Specialist in Collaborative Divorce. She developed the Rapid Advance Process, a standardized five-session brief model of counseling that was presented at the American Counseling Association convention in Atlanta in 1997 and with Vicki Carpel Miller in Honolulu in 2008. Ellie is the author of **The Bridge To I Am**, a self-help book outlining the *Rapid Advance Process* used in the treatment of Vicarious Trauma and other life challenges. Ellie hosted a call-in radio show in Phoenix and served as Self-Help Editor for a nationally syndicated trade magazine. She runs several ongoing groups called the Encouragers where people meet to offer each other peace, support and acceptance. She is Co-Director of the Vicarious Trauma Institute and the Collaborative Divorce Institute, based in Scottsdale, Arizona.

Vicki Carpel Miller, BSN, MS, LMFT

Vicki Carpel Miller is a licensed Marriage and Family Therapist in clinical practice for over 20 years. She is co-founder and Co-Director of the Vicarious Trauma Institute and the Collaborative Divorce Institute, both located in Scottsdale, Arizona. Vicki was instrumental in bringing Collaborative Divorce to Arizona and functions as a Divorce Coach and Child Specialist in Collaborative Divorce cases. She specializes in the treatment of Vicarious Trauma, the Rapid Advance Process, the practice of Collaborative Divorce and other divorce-related issues such as blended family and stepfamily issues. Vicki is internationally recognized as a trainer with the Collaborative Divorce Training Team, the Collaborative Divorce Institute and the Vicarious Trauma Institute. Her offices are located in Scottsdale, Arizona.

Ellie and Vicki opened the **Vicarious Trauma Institute** in 2006 in Arizona.

ACKNOWLEDGMENTS

We believe it is an honor and a privilege to acknowledge the dedication of the people in the helping professions. It is our professional responsibility to talk about and approach this sensitive subject with courage and forthrightness, in the hope that others will follow. We want to offer help to the helpers.

We are grateful to those who have come before us and whose work we have found invaluable in writing this book. The pioneering work of Pearlman, Saavkitne, Figley, Begley, Carl, Joseph, Weingarten, MacIan, and Wilson has provided a strong foundation of research about this subject. It is likely we have left out some important contributors. Failure to acknowledge or cite these important works at any point in the book was simply an oversight. We apologize and ask your forgiveness.

We thank all who have contributed their stories to this book. For their protection and the safety of their clients, names, place, and content have been changed.

Most importantly, we acknowledge our families and our friends who have suffered the effects of Vicarious Trauma with us and have supported us in our healing and in the writing of this manuscript. Your understanding, patience, compassion and love have been and remain life-sustaining.

Ellie and Vicki

INTRODUCTION

We have roughly estimated there to be over one hundred million *helping* professionals worldwide – those who engage in an action that benefits others at a cost to self. That is a lot of people. Hard work and dedication can take a heavy toll on the *helper*. The cost of helping others cannot really be assessed by the naked eye. Perhaps that is why so little has been written or done about it. In truth, the toll for many *helpers* is high and the amount of recovery resources is low.

This book is written for anyone in the helping professions – mental health, legal, law enforcement, clergy, teachers, and countless other professions – with the purpose of helping you recognize, address, and recover from vicarious trauma and then continuously maintain a healthy lifestyle.

Even though you are well-trained and complete continuing education on a regular basis, we fear you remain unconscious and uneducated about the signs and symptoms associated with Vicarious Trauma. Intrusive imagery, cynicism, poor memory, isolation, volatile moods, irrational fears, lack of spiritedness, physical problems or symptoms are noticed but ultimately disregarded or attributed to other better known diagnoses. How many times have you heard people ask, "How do you do this all day every day?" If you think about it, it really isn't strange to anyone that listening to trauma stories every day all day takes a heavy toll on your emotional, mental, physical and spiritual well-being.

We ourselves have frequently returned home from a long week of helping others only to discover that we are in a negatively altered emotional and physiological state. We too have endured our share of sleepless nights, elevated anxieties, periods of depression and physical ailments. We have heard our families and friends complain that we are impatient, distant and estranged from them. We too have suffered. We are not ashamed to admit it. That is why we have written this book.

It is troubling to us that most ethical codes do not mention the welfare of the *helping* professional when discussing Vicarious Trauma. We believe and we hope you agree that it is downright dangerous to continue to revere the image of the dedicated, self-sacrificing workers who never give a care to their own needs. This view perpetuates the unvoiced epidemic of Vicarious Trauma. We believe it is severely underreported in our population. We trust there are a lot of us out there suffering in silence.

The welfare of the *helping* professional for him/herself is an ever increasing issue of ethical importance. Professional Boards advocate self-care. Self-care implies that the individual is responsible for preventing the problem when it does occur. Professional *helpers* often get blamed in very shaming ways for stress responses, rather than being encouraged to see stress as a natural response and as an opportunity for introspection and feedback. We truly believe that our approach will maintain and strengthen the clear and good judgment of the *helping* professional and therefore, may well be the best way to serve the client, patient, or person.

CHAPTER ONE

Where There's Smoke, There's Fire

We have all heard of second-hand smoke. What image does that conjure up for you? Let us put you in a room with a heavy smoker. You are breathing in the smoky air. As you inhale, it irritates your nose, your mouth, your lungs, your bloodstream. It smells and remains on your skin, your hair and your clothes. After a while, you might start wheezing or coughing and your eyes may become irritated. Then, it may be difficult to breathe. Prolonged exposure creates a greater risk for adversely affecting your health and well being, perhaps causing damage to your heart and your brain. Inhaling smoke over time may cause you to develop asthma, emphysema, chronic pulmonary disorder, cancer and the like. Let's look at how the experience of absorbing trauma "second-hand" is equally as dangerous.

The experience of absorbing trauma, second-hand, is much the same as the second-hand smoke example. The person who experiences the primary trauma may be adversely affected by a syndrome called Post Traumatic Stress Disorder. The primary trauma survivor is the one who was in the car accident, at the disaster, caught in the storm, fighting the war, or being abandoned by a parent, a spouse, or suffering the rape, the robbery or the attack. They are having the event happen to them. The heroes who are called upon to help, listen, observe, intervene, guide and care are exposed to that same trauma, second-hand, and over time are at risk for something we call Second-Hand Shock Syndrome.

We believe that Second-Hand Shock Syndrome is spectrum disorder that encompasses a wide range of physical, emotional, cognitive and spiritual effects from the indirect experience of trauma much like being in the presence of a smoker creates Second-hand smoke. Over time, this can indirectly create disease in its recipient. The effects of trauma are contagious, adversely affecting your body, mind and spirit.

An Epidemic?

We believe that there are many millions of people struggling with some form of Second-Hand Shock Syndrome – both professional and lay persons. We are all exposed to trauma daily, many times a day. The news, radio talk shows, instant information via the Internet continue to feed us copious doses of *trauma content* while we have little consciousness of the fact that we are even being traumatized, much less what the *trauma content* is doing to our health and well-being.

When we are first indirectly exposed to trauma, our brain begins to paint a picture for us by the activation of mirror neurons in the visual cortex. We see the event as if it were happening to us. A series of bio-physiological events then occur which results in the spilling out of chemicals into our bloodstream and throughout our body. This ultimately concludes in the over-production of cortisol that contributes to the onset of many serious physical illnesses.

We believe people are currently being treated for the symptoms of Second-Hand Shock Syndrome, which can be confused as other illnesses. We think Second-Hand Shock Syndrome needs to be addressed and treated as its own illness. Folks are treated for arthritis, cancer, heart disease, obesity, anxiety and depression who likely began their downhill descent with some form of Second-Hand Shock Syndrome. We think it needs to become a recognized diagnosis and we believe that if people began to recognize the chronic intrusion of *trauma content* in their lives that their physical health would improve. It would also save our ailing healthcare system billions of dollars.

A Diagnosis

The serious diagnosis of Second-Hand Shock Syndrome is being missed. We believe there are three dimensions to this syndrome: **Compassion Fatigue**, **Secondary Traumatic Stress** and **Vicarious Trauma**.

Second-Hand Shock Syndrome is a spectrum disorder that encompasses differing levels of compassion fatigue, secondary traumatic stress and vicarious trauma. We do not even begin to assume how to develop the exact relationship between these three disorders, but we believe they are all related and overlap to some degree. For the purposes of this book, we will focus on the topic of Vicarious Trauma since we believe that *helpers* mostly suffer in silence as the onset of Vicarious Trauma is slow, subtle and covert.

SECOND-HAND SHOCK SYNDROME

Historically, the terms Compassion Fatigue or Burnout, Secondary Traumatic Stress and Vicarious Trauma have been used synonymously as if they all have the same meaning. We disagree. While we believe there is significant overlap between them, we see them with defining differences.

Compassion Fatigue (Burnout) can be defined as long-term exhaustion and diminished interest in one's work. It typically includes the lessening of compassion over time as a result of the taxing nature of extending compassion to those in need.

Charles

> *Charles was an adolescent counselor in practice for about thirty years. He must have heard every story in the book, because it truly showed. Nothing surprised him or fazed him anymore. In fact, sometimes when a client was recounting an upsetting event, Charles would remark to the client, "Oh, that's nothing new. I've heard that one a hundred times already". Sometimes he would daze off into space when a client was speaking. A few times, he even fell asleep. When the client asked if he was sleeping, he answered, "Of course not, I was contemplating your issue". At that point Charles thought he'd better do something about his apparent apathy, insensitivity and disinterest in his work.*

We can define Secondary Traumatic Stress as the natural consequent behaviors and emotions that result from knowledge of another's traumatic experience (Figley, 1995). Here is an example of Secondary Traumatic Stress.

Wendy

Wendy was rudely awakened at 2 a.m. by the telephone. Peter was on the line, sobbing and babbling senselessly. As Wendy brushed the sleep from her eyes, she tried to tune into Peter's ranting. "Peter, slow down. I can't understand you. What in heaven's name is wrong?" Peter slowly got hold of himself and blurted out, "Sandra just packed up and left me. She told me she's been having an affair for a nearly two years. I just want to kill myself!"

Wendy thought for a moment, jumped out of bed, and ran next door. She then spent the rest of the night and the wee hours of the morning listening to her friend's husband unveil the sordid details of his unhappy marriage. Wendy spent a long night with Peter. She cried with him, got angry at her friend, questioned her friend's decision and commiserated with Peter throughout the night.

By morning, Peter was calmer, no longer thinking of taking his life, and called his therapist for assistance. After that, he called a lawyer.

Wendy went home drained and exhausted. She was shocked by her friend's behavior and lack of disclosure about the affair. Peter leaned on Wendy for quite a while during the transition of his divorce. Wendy noticed that she didn't feel quite herself during this time and within a short time began to struggle with insomnia and depression. She started to feel more and more disturbed not only about her friend but about her own marriage. Was she safe from this kind of betrayal? Was her marriage solid? Could she and her husband be heading for this same disastrous road? She struggled to regulate the upsetting emotions she was experiencing until she tabled it somewhere in the recesses of her mind.

Wendy was a "first responder" to a traumatic event. Even though we don't typically think of a friend or neighbor as a first responder, they are sometimes called upon to fulfill this important role and they can be negatively affected by it. Wendy could automatically let out her upset and did not have a need to control her response to Peter's primary trauma. The option to express her empathy automatically and passionately helped her to partially deal with the content. Expressing her empathy automatically is what differentiates Secondary Traumatic Stress from Vicarious Trauma.

As an aside, we frequently hear about the plight of first responders. They are our heroes because they are there to rescue the endangered, the suffering and the needy and they are there to help us whenever we are unsafe or in need. We believe that there are many more heroes who fit into the category of a first responder. We believe first responders include many types of *helpers*, more than the first responder we stereotypically think of when we come up with that phrase.

How many times do we find ourselves in crisis and choose to turn to a friend or other loved one? That friend is a first responder, like Wendy. Can you imagine picking up the phone after being served a summons and wanting to talk to anyone else other than your lawyer? She or he is a first responder. We believe that anyone can fit in the category of first responder to someone else. All of these people are our heroes. Sometimes a first responder is a friend, military personnel, a counselor, or a clergy member. Sometimes the first responder is a lawyer, a judge, a doctor, hospice worker, a journalist, a teacher, an insurance adjustor, the 911 operator. Anyone who gives us help or good advice is our hero. Anyone who listens in another's time of need is at risk for Second-Hand Shock Syndrome.

Vicarious Trauma is in its own league because this disorder includes not only having to be compassionate while listening to the *trauma content* stories of others, it also includes straining one's brain in an attempt to control the listener's empathic response to the traumatic event. An example of someone struggling with Vicarious Trauma will follow shortly. Take a look at the table to see how similar the symptoms are:

As you can see, the symptoms of these disorders can be similar to each other. Many of them mirror the symptoms associated with Post Traumatic Stress Disorder. Let's try to clarify some of the characteristics that differentiate these three conditions. If you are feeling less compassionate than usual in your work, if your apathy level is up, you may have Compassion Fatigue. If beyond that, you experience intrusive thoughts, bad dreams or depression, anxiety, insomnia, recurring infections or unexplained illnesses, you may have Secondary Traumatic Stress. If you have a vocation of listening and needing to control your empathic response in addition to the above listed characteristics, symptomologies or criteria, you may very well have Vicarious Trauma.

Post Traumatic Stress Disorder	Compassion Fatigue
Stressor: Experienced an event outside the range of usual human experience that would be markedly distressing to almost anyone. • Serious threat to self • Sudden destruction of one's environment	**Stressor: Experienced repeated situations where the sole responsibility is to care.** • Serious threat to a traumatized person • Sudden destruction of the traumatized persons environment • Chronic, repeated exposure to situations where listening and empathizing with upset people is required
Re-experiencing the Trauma event. • Recollections of the event • Dreams of the event • Sudden re-experience of the event • Reminders of the distressing event	**Re-experiencing the Trauma event.** • Recollections of the event/traumatized person • Dreams of the event or the traumatized person • Sudden re-experience of the event or the traumatized person • Reminders of the traumatized person/distressing event
Avoidance/Numbing of reminders of the event. • Efforts to avoid thoughts and feelings • Efforts to avoid activities or situations • Psychogenic amnesia • Diminished interest in activities • Detachment / estrangement from others • Diminished affect • Sense of foreshortened future	**Avoidance/Numbing of reminders of the event.** • Efforts to avoid thoughts and feelings • Efforts to avoid activities or situations • Psychogenic amnesia • Diminished interest in activities • Detachment / estrangement from others • Diminished affect • Sense of foreshortened future
Persistent Arousal • Insomnia • Irritability or outbursts of anger • Difficulty concentrating • Hypervigilance for self • Exaggerated startle response • Physiologic reactivity to cues	**Persistent Numbing for self-preservation** • Insomnia • Distractibility • Difficulty concentrating • Lack of interest in work • Feelings of dread

Adapted from Figley, 1995

Secondary Traumatic Stress	Vicarious Trauma
Stressor: Experienced an event outside the range of usual human experience that would be markedly distressing to almost anyone. • Serious threat to a traumatized person • Sudden destruction of the traumatized persons environment	**Stressor: Experienced an event outside the range of usual human experience that would be markedly distressing to almost anyone** • Serious threat to a traumatized person • Sudden destruction of the traumatized persons environment • Straining to repeatedly control one's empathic response
Re-experiencing the Trauma event. • Recollections of the event/traumatized person • Dreams of the event or the traumatized person • Sudden re-experience of the event or the traumatized person • Reminders of the traumatized person/distressing event	**Re-experiencing the Trauma event.** • Recollections of the event/traumatized person • Dreams of the event or the traumatized person • Sudden re-experience of the event or the traumatized person • Reminders of the traumatized person/distressing event
Avoidance/Numbing of reminders of the event. • Efforts to avoid thoughts and feelings • Efforts to avoid activities or situations • Psychogenic amnesia • Diminished interest in activities • Detachment / estrangement from others • Diminished affect • Sense of foreshortened future	**Avoidance/Numbing of reminders of the event.** • Efforts to avoid thoughts and feelings • Efforts to avoid activities or situations • Psychogenic amnesia • Diminished interest in activities • Detachment / estrangement from others • Diminished affect • Sense of foreshortened future
Persistent Arousal • Insomnia • Irritability or outbursts of anger • Difficulty concentrating • Hypervigilance for the traumatized person • Exaggerated startle response • Physiologic reactivity to cues	**Persistent Arousal** • Insomnia • Irritability or outbursts of anger • Difficulty concentrating • Hypervigilance for the traumatized person • Exaggerated startle response • Physiologic reactivity to cues

Adapted from Figley, 1995

Internalizing trauma can cause obesity, immune disorders, cancer, endocrine imbalance, digestive problems, depression, anxiety, and brain damage. A wide range of human illness can all be attributed to the effects of ongoing trauma on the human brain and body.

We will be looking more closely at Vicarious Trauma for the remainder of this book because we believe that this syndrome is screaming for contribution from others. We need research, empirical work and help for the professional *helper*. Professional *helpers* are our heroes and without them our ability to cope with life's daily trauma would diminish. Our heroes absorb trauma more intensely because they help for a living.

We consider this book as a gateway into the realm of increased knowledge regarding human health and well being. And if you are a *helping* professional, you not only take in the trauma of television, violent movies and video games, talk radio, terrorism, war, financial ruin, and fears of attack, but you also listen to *trauma content stories* all day every day while you control your empathic response. This can be a deadly combo.

CHAPTER TWO

A Serious Situation

Anna, Paralegal

Anna, a 40-year-old woman, came to counseling for hypnotherapy. Her presenting problem was a recently developed fear of flying. She had flown often for her paralegal job of seventeen years, which included traveling to different states and gathering information for depositions. The phobia had become so bad, even the thought of buying a ticket triggered a panic attack. Her law firm represented plaintiffs in medical malpractice and other wrongful death lawsuits. Some of these suits pertained to accidental deaths in airplane crashes. She developed her flying phobia just about the time she was gathering evidence in a wrongful death suit involving a small private jet.

Anna heard many traumatic stories and studied numerous vivid, disturbing pictures over the length of her career. She would write lengthy motions and memos that were filled with graphic details of death, severe illness and mutilation. She described her role in the firm as the "empathy agent". She was always the first contact with whom the client would share their appalling story. Anna listened to the clients' narrative as if it were happening to her. She would share the clients' pain and demonstrate her compassion for the client. She was also very good at her job and brought in huge settlements for the client and the firm.

After further questioning, it was revealed that this married mother of two also suffered from depression, irritability, emotional numbness and insomnia. She described herself as "robotic" – going to work every day and coming home every evening only to place herself in front of the TV to watch Crime Scene Investigation. She isolated herself from the outside world and barely interacted with her family. She reported that she had no tolerance for the day-to-day troubles of her growing children and often reacted to them with anger and impatience. Small issues were eliciting high levels of anxiety and she was becoming hypervigilant about not getting injured. Activities that were commonplace for her such as driving, swimming, shopping all evoked a fear response. Anna started to sob as she mumbled that there was no happiness or meaning in her life anymore and the world was an awful place to be. Anna had a lot more to deal with than a flying phobia, she was suffering from Vicarious Trauma.

What is Vicarious Trauma? The technical definition of Vicarious Trauma is a permanent transformation in the *helper's* inner experience resulting from empathic engagement with the client's traumatic material (Pearlman, Saakvitne, & Figley, 1995). More simply put, Vicarious Trauma is a set of cognitive, emotional, physical and spiritual disturbances that result from helping trauma survivors. Every time a *helper* interacts with a client, he or she is putting him or herself at risk. All of us are secondary witnesses to trauma nearly every day. All we need to do is watch television, listen to or read the news. A traumatic response in any one individual is the result of a number of processes, some of them biological, some of them psychological. It is also important to remember that any experience of trauma is in the "eye" of the beholder. There are cultural, historical and childhood frames of reference that may help one person go into a trauma response when it will not affect another in quite the same way (International Trauma Consultants, 2006).

Vicarious Trauma is more than Secondary Traumatic Stress, which is defined as indirect exposure to trauma through a firsthand account or narrative of a traumatic event. Vicarious Trauma is a part of a syndrome that anyone in the *helping* position can experience. It is characterized by a painful set of symptoms that result from utilizing controlled empathy while listening to or seeing traumatic narrative content (Wilson & Thomas, 2004).

Controlled empathy, by itself, is a vigorous neurological activity. When a *helping* person is listening to the shocking, sad, or awful stories of another, it may look like he or she is calmly sitting and listening. But the activity going on inside the listener's brain and body looks anything but calm. Not only is the *helper* absorbing the shocking story, he or she must respond to the content in a constrained manner that is geared to helping the suffering person. If you are or know someone in the *helping* professions, it is useful for you to understand the neuroscience of controlled empathy. It is important to note that controlled empathy and automatic empathy are not the same. Neurologically, they travel in different circuitries in your brain (International Trauma

Consultants, 2006). Because controlled empathy is automatic empathy interrupted, it casts a much greater strain on physiology, emotions and spiritual well being.

So, what is automatic empathy? The neurological activity of automatic empathy involves a specific system of neurons called mirror neurons. The process forms a neurological loop originating from the mirror neurons in the pre-frontal cortices of the brain and traveling throughout different regions of the brain. This neurological loop creates in the listener a full body sensation as if the listener is actually experiencing the event. The neurons form a specific brain circuitry that underlies the empathic impulse and ultimately helps the listener to adopt another's point of view. This circuitry sets the stage of the human imagination: it is a right brain activity and the *helper* imagines the event as if it were happening to him or her (Wilson & Thomas, 2004).

Researchers studied the empathic response by locating the neurons in the anterior cingulae of the brain that respond to a patient being poked with a needle. These neurons are referred to as sensory neurons. Remarkably, these researchers also found that some of these neurons fire with equal strength when the patient watches someone else being poked. When this type of sensory neuron is fired, changes take place throughout the body as if the witness is having the pain. New brain scan techniques have enabled scientists to prove that the ability to empathize is an intrinsic part of the brain. Empathy neurons dissolve the barrier between the self and the other (Kramer, 2007).

Empathy, the ability to share another's emotions, is rooted in infancy. For example, newborn babies will cry in response to the cries of another infant (Kramer 2007). Early in life we learn to imitate – matching emotions to expressions and events. We use that information to predict each other's emotions and act compassionately or vicariously, depending on the situation.

A pattern of the brain strain associated with controlled empathy is observed starting with the activation of the visual cortex. As the listener hears the revolting story, he or she begins to visualize it in the mind as if it is actually happening. The brain is struggling with another's upset. In this process, called controlled empathy, the *helper* has to rev up his or her internal resources to remain calm (International Trauma Consultants, 2006). This activity taxes the right hemisphere of the brain because impulses from the activated mirror neurons want to surge from it, but the *helper* has to hold back because he or she needs to remain controlled. Imagine yourself setting a top spinning, and then, needing to immediately interrupt its gyrations. It's like going against a force of nature.

Dora, Psychotherapist

An 8-year-old girl was brought to therapy by her maternal grandparents. She was experiencing night terrors for three months. Her father was incarcerated three years ago and her mother had passed away. This was the only information given to me at the time I made the appointment by telephone. I was curious to find out how this child was so dramatically abandoned by her parents. The grandmother insisted that she meet with me prior to my taking a session alone with the child. Here is what she told me. When the little girl was four years old, her parents separated. "My daughter was a beautiful person, a model and she had a beautiful heart. My son-in-law was an abuser, but in disguise. No one believed that a man of his sophistication and stature in the community could be so evil and violent. My daughter asked for a divorce and in the beginning of that process we thought he was going to cooperate. But his anger was only building and he was determined to take little Maya away from her mother. My daughter reported all of the minor incidents of domestic violence to the police, but none were deemed severe enough for the police to take action. One day, when Maya was at school, he intruded into my daughter's place of business, doused her with gasoline and lit her on fire." At this point the grandmother was weeping and I had to repress my own natural gag reflex. The grandmother continued to share that her daughter held on for about thirty-six hours after the horrific incident. She said that the screams of agony coming out of the burn unit were blood curdling. After telling the police that it was her husband who perpetrated the act, she died. All I keep thinking about is that now Maya has no mother, and a father who will never be released from prison. The grand- mother has lost her only daughter. She wanted Maya to get help for the intense trauma she sustained. I am giving this help, but it is exacting a painful toll on my own well being.

When a person engages in automatic empathy, rather than controlled empathy, he or she can let out the tension freely. This process, which we will call Secondary Trau- matic Stress, has a less negative physiological impact on the brain. The right brain and left brain work together to resolve the process of automatic empathy. The brain activity of a person experiencing automatic empathy, a healthy neurological process, is much like the top, spinning until it slows down and then stops on its own. Once the left and right brain have once again achieved a calm balance, or homeostasis, the empathic person has the ability to respond to the story and more easily access higher mind dynamics for helping. These dynamics might include forgiveness, hope, faith, and courage. These spiritually-based dynamics are so important to utilize in traumatic situations.

Empathy plays a critical role in many facets of life, from management and sales to friendship and parenting and to the many dimensions of the *helping* professions. It leads the way to compassion, moral awareness and spiritual well-being. When the complicated neurological activity of controlled empathy is coupled with the neurological strain of traumatic content, people are faced with the probability of suffering Vicarious Trauma, a subset of Second-Hand Shock Syndrome.

(Use of the term Second-Hand Shock Syndrome is solely the opinion of the authors and has not been researched or identified as a syndrome in the general mental health literature at this time.)

CHAPTER THREE

The Neuroscience of Trauma

The biological effects of Vicarious Trauma fall into a range of trauma categories that researchers distinguish from one another, although there is not necessarily agreement about how to do this. We have attempted to do this in the preceding chapter and recognize that much more research needs to be developed in the evolving diagnosis of Second-Hand Shock Syndrome. We assume that the subject of trauma will continue to undergo many transitions. One thing that much of the research maintains is that the terms *shock, stress response, trauma response, acute stress disorder, acute* or *chronic post traumatic stress disorder, burnout, compassion fatigue* and *vicarious trauma* all have stress in common. Stress is an alarm reaction to a stimulus the person appraises as emotionally charged or threatening. This state can range from exhilaration to mild or severe discomfort. We believe that trauma is stress run amok. Understanding the movement from stress into trauma demands a basic understanding of the structure of the brain.

The brain is structured into three main parts, long observed in autopsies:

1) The cortex which includes the outer surface, where higher, rational thinking and spiritual skills arise. This includes the frontal cortex, which is the most recently evolved portion;

2) The limbic system which is the center of the brain where emotions are triggered; and

3) The brain stem which contains the reptilian brain that controls basic survival functions (Healing Resources Info, 2005).

Stress originates in the amygdala, which is in the mid-brain, and is also called the primitive or limbic brain. This is the dwelling place of the fight, flight or freeze reaction. It produces hyper-arousal, a normal and necessary response to threat. The fight or flight and/or freeze reactions prepare the body for defensive acts through a cascade of sympathetic nervous system firings and the release of stress hormones, the most well known of which are epinephrine and adrenaline. Our physical reactions match the potential demands on us. Our pupils dilate so we can sense what is going on around us. Our skin conductivity intensifies so that the hair on our skin will stand up and we can sense vibration. The heart's output increases so that more blood is pumped to the extremities, readying our arms and legs to run if necessary. Our respiratory rate intensifies as more oxygen is provided for our tissues. At the same time, blood is diverted from the digestive system, producing the sensation of gnawing in the stomach. Once the perceived danger is passed, the body halts the alarm reaction and restores the body to homeostasis or a state of rest (Weingarten, 2003). Thus, the body ratchets up for defense and then must ratchet down for recovery.

Stress throws our nervous system out of whack but only for a short period of time. Within a few days or weeks our nervous system calms down and we revert to a normal state of equilibrium. This return to normalcy is not the case when we are being traumatized. Trauma stress can be distinguished from routine stress by assessing the following:

1. How quickly the upset is triggered;

2. How frequently the upset is triggered;

3. How intensely threatening the source of the upset is;

4. How long the upset lasts; and

5. How long it takes to calm down (Healing Resources Info, 2005).

If we feel frozen, or, conversely, if we feel in a state of active emotional intensity, we are experiencing emotional trauma even though we may not be consciously aware of the level of distress. Trauma actually changes the structure of the brain at the point where the frontal cortex, the emotional brain, and the survival brain converge. One significant finding is that the brain scans of people with relationship or developmental problems, or learning and social problems related to emotional intelligence, reveal similar structural and functional irregularities as individuals suffering from Post Traumatic Stress Disorder (Healing Resources Info, 2005).

Post Traumatic Stress Disorder was originally categorized as a set of symptoms incurred as a result of experiencing traumatic or life-threatening events. Such events originally included:

- natural disasters;
- wartime events;
- horrific accidents or crimes; and
- experiencing or witnessing horrific injury or fatalities.

Other potential sources of trauma that are often overlooked and that we include within Second-Hand Shock Syndrome include:

- falls or sports injuries;
- surgery, particularly emergency surgery;
- serious illness;
- birth trauma;
- hearing about violence or the death of someone close.

In addition, traumatic stress that influences the brain is caused by:

- poor relationships with primary caregivers;
- forced separation very early in life;
- chronic misattunement of caregiver to the child's attachment signals, for reasons such as physical or mental illness, depression, or grief.

Recent research also suggests that early life trauma creates vulnerability and higher risk for experiencing future traumatic responses (Healing Resources Info, 2005). Research reveals that emotional trauma can result from such common occurrences as:

- an auto accident;
- the breakup of a significant relationship;
- a disappointing or deeply humiliating experience; and
- the discovery of a life threatening illness, or a disabling condition.

Traumatizing events can take a serious toll on those involved, even if the event did not cause physical damage. Emotional trauma contains three elements:

- it was unexpected;
- the person was unprepared; and
- there was nothing the person could directly do to prevent the event from happening (Healing Resources Info, 2005).

Remember, it is not the event itself that determines whether something is traumatic to an individual, but their perception of the experience. Also, remember that how a person will react to a particular event is not predictable. For someone who is used to being in control of emotions and events, it may be surprising, even embarrassing, to discover that something like job loss can be so debilitating. It is important to recognize that some people are more resilient than others. Resiliency studies demonstrate that resilience is developed in early childhood when the child learns in a positive way to overcome the challenges of life. Many *helpers* have not learned positive resiliency skills. Research shows that more than 53% of *helpers* are adult survivors of some type of childhood abuse. Abused children don't learn resilience. They grow up to be even more vulnerable to the effects of Second-Hand-Shock Syndrome. The abuse drives them into professions that expose them to more trauma.

Repetitive recall of traumatic memories and chronic intermittent hyperarousal are characteristic of Post Traumatic Stress. Hyperarousal and memory dysfunction implicate the limbic brain regions, including the amygdaloidal complex, hippocampal formation and limbic cortex, such as the orbit frontal and anterior cingualae areas (Liberzon, Taylor, Amdur, Jung, Chamberlin, Minoshima, & Fig, 1999). Many areas of the brain are activated and involved when experiencing a traumatic event.

Limbic System

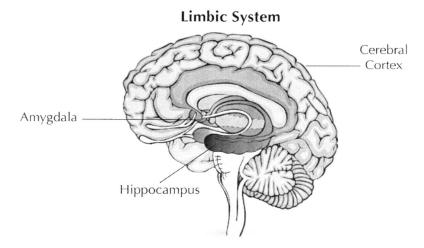

The neuroscience of trauma can also be discussed by considering the structure in the brain stem called the locus coeruleus. It has many connections throughout the brain to activate and alert a person, even interrupting the individual if necessary, to ensure that attention is paid to high priority stimuli. When a person is repeatedly exposed to a threat, or exposed to an extreme threat, the locus coeruleus actually changes; it becomes hyper responsive to stress signals (Weingarten, 2003). This produces the felt experience of hyper-vigilance for the individual; in effect, the locus coeruleus itself suffers trauma or brain damage. The hyper responsiveness of this part of the brain sets the primitive brain working in overdrive while the higher brain functions less. The victim feels stressed and tense much of the time.

The limbic system also plays a key role in the body's response to trauma. The amygdala assigns emotional significance to incoming signals and the hippocampus evaluates, categorizes and stores information. Coordination between both structures is paramount for normal functioning. One reacts to incoming information and the other makes sense of it. Under conditions of extreme stress, an agitated amygdala interferes with and could shut down the hippocampus, resulting in a number of symptoms that are associated with the long-term effects of trauma such as memory loss and intrusive imagery.

Under extreme stress, the amygdala takes charge of the experience and expression of fear. It will forge conditions between the elements, e.g., heart rate, respiratory rate, blood pressure, in the threatening situation and a fear response without the individual having any awareness that it is even happening. Thus, a person may be left with a fear response to triggers in the environment that actually make no sense to him or her (Weingarten, 2003). Furthermore, neurons have a lot of difficulty in forging connections to the higher mind where forgiving, hopeful and peaceful thinking is accessed.

The more the brain has to deal with, the more it will adapt and change. Eventually these adaptations can become maladaptive. People who have been repeatedly exposed to the most troubling kinds of interactions and events and who have worked diligently to meet these challenges may find that they respond with heightened reactivity and feel overwhelmed a great deal of the time. This sensitization creates mountains out of molehills. Small issues that would typically not bother others present major upsets for the affected person. Children and adults who have been exposed to domestic abuse are a particularly vulnerable group in this area and have frequently been found to be suffering from Post Traumatic Stress Disorder (Healing Resources Info, 2005).

The relationship between any traumatic emotional stress, hippocampus injury, memory loss, and traumatic amnesia has been examined. This relationship has been well-documented and it has been demonstrated that animals and humans exposed to high levels of stress, fear and arousal for prolonged periods commonly experience learning deficits and memory loss ranging from the minimal to the profound (Schore, 2003).

As stress and arousal levels increase, learning and memory decrease in accordance with the classic u-shaped curve. These memory deficits are due to disturbances in hippocampus activation and arousal and in the corticosteroid secretion that can suppress neural activity associated with learning and memory, thereby inducing hippocampus atrophy. Trauma can induce disturbances in all aspects of spiritual, social and emotional functioning and affect the growth and survival of dendrites, axons, synapses, inter-neurons and neurons, all of which essential for healthy brain functioning (Joseph, 1999).

With the significant neurological information presented above, it is evident and should be frightening to note that trauma, in whatever form, is a high-risk neurological event and can result in permanent damage to the brain and create extremely painful consequences for its victim.

CHAPTER FOUR

The Psychology of Trauma

The mental health response to trauma has undergone enormous change in the last decade. Trauma psychology has become a field of study and treatment in and of itself. Acute Stress Disorder was not included until the Diagnostic and Statistical Manual of Mental Disorders IV was published. This came about due to those involved in crisis intervention repeatedly pointing out the need for a conceptual classification that addressed the traumatic event in the first few weeks of stress, and not just Post Traumatic Stress Disorder after the first month. The classification also served the practical purpose of providing insurance coverage. The most current version of the DSM is the Fourth Edition, Text Revision (DSM-IV-TR; 2000). The DSM V is not expected to appear until 2011, or later (Baldwin, 2007).

Linking acute stress and early interventions along a continuum that recognized the need for ongoing and long term intervention for individuals who did develop Post Traumatic Stress Disorder was the purpose of using the term Trauma Psychology as an umbrella term to describe this evolving specialty. Trauma Psychology includes short term crisis intervention, sometimes referred to as Critical Incident Stress Management (Carll, 2007).

In its original sense, trauma involves exposure to a life-threatening experience. This fits with its phylogenetic roots in life-or-death issues of survival as pointed out in the previous chapter. Yet, people who have been exposed to violations by individuals or institutions they must depend on or trust also show symptoms similar to those caused by Post Traumatic Stress Disorder, even if their abuse was not directly life threatening (Lee, 2006). Trauma experiences shake the foundations of our beliefs about safety and shatter our assumptions of trust. They can break the spirit of an individual and set that person up to forget the power of faith. Because these events are perceived so far outside of what we would expect, they provoke reactions that feel strange and crazy. Even though the reactions appear unusual and disturbing, they are actually characteristic and quite common. Trauma symptoms are probably adaptive and originally evolved to help us recognize and avoid dangerous situations quickly, before it is too late. Sometimes these symptoms resolve within a few days or weeks of a disturbing experience. Not everyone who experiences a traumatic event will develop Post Traumatic Stress Disorder. We create meaning out of the context in which events occur. Consequently, there is always a strong subjective component in people's responses to traumatic events (Baldwin, 2007).

How is it that an event can cause an emotionally traumatic response in one person and not another? Let's take a closer look at this phenomenon. We already mentioned that trauma is in the "eye" of the beholder and many factors affect an individual's particular experience of a traumatic event and their ability to be resilient. Some of the factors involved are the:

- severity of the event;
- individual's history, which may not even be recalled;
- larger meaning the event represents for the individual, which may or may not be immediately evident;
- coping skills, values, beliefs, spiritual views held by individuals, some of which may have never been identified; and
- reactions and support from family, friends and professionals (Baldwin, 2007).

Post Traumatic Stress Disorder is officially classified as an anxiety disorder, but some have argued that it fits more closely with the dissociative disorders. Others feel it belongs by itself. There has also been some discussion over differential diagnoses for simple vs. chronic traumatic histories such as Complex Post Traumatic Stress Disorder, or the proposed DESNOS diagnosis (Disorders of Extreme Stress, Not Otherwise Specified). Recent work suggests that DESNOS may be more frequent among individuals whose subsequent adult traumas complicate chronic or unresolved childhood traumatic experiences, and that DESNOS has important implications for treatment (Baldwin, 2007). Classification issues such as these will probably continue through field trials for the DSM-V. We are hopeful that our suggestion for Second-Hand Shock Syndrome be carefully considered as a viable possibility.

Common effects or conditions may occur following a traumatic event. Sometimes these responses can be delayed for months or even years after the event. Often, people do not even initially associate their symptoms with the precipitating trauma. Symptoms are more likely to result from a commonplace trauma such as surgery or a minor car accident, if there were earlier, overwhelming life experiences. This may result from state-dependent learning, in which previous responses to a terrifying event are repeated even though more appropriate response could be used, such as proactive defenses that would enable parents to help their hurt child rather than freeze (Baldwin, 2007). These defenses fit into three categories: physical, emotional and cognitive. The following chart is condensed from the writings of Jaffe, Segal, and Dumke (2005):

PHYSICAL	EMOTIONAL	COGNITIVE
Eating Disturbances	Depression, despair	Memory Lapse
Sleep Disturbances	Anxiety, Panic Attacks	Difficulty making decisions
Sexual Dysfunction	Fearfulness	Decreased ability to concentrate
Low energy	OCD behaviors	Feeling Distracted
Chronic unexplained pain	Irritability, Anger	ADHD Symptoms
	Emotional numbness	

Additional symptoms can occur with a severe precipitating event and also as a delayed reaction. One set of symptoms is categorized as re-experiencing the trauma and includes:

- intrusive thoughts,
- flashbacks,
- nightmares, and
- sudden flood of emotion or images related to the event.

Another set of symptoms is categorized as emotional numbing and avoidance. It includes:

- amnesia;
- avoidance of situations that resemble the initial event;
- detachment;
- guilt feelings;
- grief reaction;
- altered sense of time;
- increased arousal;
- hypervigilance, jumpiness, or extreme sense of being on guard;
- overreactions, including sudden unprovoked anger;
- general anxiety;
- obsessions with death; and
- insomnia (Jaffe et al., 2005).

When unrecognized, emotional trauma persists and remains unresolved and can create lasting difficulties in an individual's life. One way to determine whether an emotional or psychological trauma has occurred is to look at the recurring problems an individual might be experiencing. These can serve as clues to an earlier situation that causes a dysregulation in the structure or the function of the brain. Common personal and behavioral effects of emotional trauma include:

- substance abuse;
- compulsive behavior patterns;
- self-destructive and impulsive behavior;
- uncontrollable reactive thoughts;
- inability to make healthy professional or lifestyle choices;
- dissociation or splitting off parts of the self;
- feelings of ineffectiveness, shame, despair; and
- a loss of previously sustained beliefs and spiritual values.

Common effects of emotional trauma on interpersonal relationships include:

- inability to maintain close relationships;
- inability to choose appropriate friends or mates;
- sexual problems;
- hostility;
- recurring arguments with family members or colleagues;
- social withdrawal; and
- feeling constantly threatened (Healing Resources and Info, 2005).

Trauma takes a huge toll on the individual and untreated, can destroy the life of its victim.

CHAPTER FIVE

When Is It Vicarious Trauma?

Anyone can be traumatized. The risk for Post Traumatic Stress Disorder increases with exposure to trauma. Chronic or multiple traumatic experiences are likely to be more difficult to overcome than most single instances. Post Traumatic Stress Disorder is also more apt to occur if passive defenses, such as freezing or dissociation are used, rather than active defenses such as fight or flight. There is some evidence that early traumatic experiences, especially if prolonged or repeated, may markedly increase the risk of developing Post Traumatic Stress Disorder after traumatic exposure as an adult (Baldwin, 2007).

Our focus now turns to the subgroup of Second-Hand Shock Syndrome – Vicarious Trauma – which includes both graphic and painful material and primarily affects workers who help trauma and disaster victims. This includes psychologists and other mental health professionals, lawyers, paralegals, judges, custody evaluators, EMTs, nurses, physicians, clergy, police, criminologists, dentists, journalists fire and rescue workers, family members, and close friends. We frequently call these people our heroes. In fact, anyone who is exposed to an overdose of *victim suffering* is at risk Secondary Traumatic Stress Disorder. If you add the component of controlled empathy, which we discussed in Chapter 2, you have Vicarious Trauma. As we previously wrote, several studies of *helping* populations show that at least 53% of *helping* professionals describe themselves as survivors of some form of childhood trauma (Perlman & Saakvitne, 1995). This historical situation increases the possibility of contracting Vicarious Trauma.

If you work with the stories of many trauma/disaster victims, be aware of three major risk factors for Vicarious Trauma:

1. exposure to the stories or images of multiple trauma victims;

2. your controlled empathic sensitivity to their suffering; and,

3. any unresolved emotional issues that relate affectively and/or symbolically to the suffering seen or heard.

Experts warn that symptoms of Vicarious Trauma should be taken seriously and steps should be taken to heal, just as you would take action to heal from a physical ailment. As with any physical condition, the amount of time or assistance needed to recover from emotional trauma varies from person to person.

Several job characteristics can fuel Vicarious Trauma:

1. cumulative impact of client trauma stories;

2. repetitive contact with troubled people;

3. intense personal contact with these people while you work with them;

4. ongoing involvement;

5. the ethical pressure of maintaining confidentiality; and

6. the giving role in general (Lee, 2007).

Untreated Vicarious Trauma can cause severe, debilitating anxiety that persists for months or even years. It can truly break the spirit of the *helper*. Because these *helpers* are not directly involved in the event, their distress often goes undetected and untreated.

Let's go back to the case study of Anna in Chapter 2. Here is the story in her words:

> *"You requested that I write about the case that affected me the most. Boy, to pick just one is tough. Numerous cases have affected my life in various ways. Tragic cases involving children are probably the toughest. In most cases, I emotionally deal with them by rationalizing that 'this could not happen to me or most people because...' One case that I will pick, however, is one that could happen to anyone. It involved a young mom in her 30's. She was a strong person who was a good wife and a good mom. She had a problem with alcohol when younger but was successfully in recovery. In 1998, she had a routine pap smear. It was performed by a doctor in Arizona but sent to a lab in New Mexico. It was read as normal. In 1999, she had another routine pap smear and it was sent to the same lab in New Mexico for interpreting. Again, it was read a*

normal. The young mom was having abnormal menstrual problems and pain. In 2001, a new pap smear revealed malignant cervical cancer. Upon investigation, it was discovered that the 1998 and 1999 slides were mis-read. Those two slides were both read by the same lab technician who was later fired. By the time the 2001 slide was read it was too late for this young mom. All radical treatments were fruitless. She would have had better than an 80% chance of recovery if the malignancy was properly discovered in 1998 or 1999. She died about one year after the 2001 slide was read after suffering horrible pain. Pictures showed that she slowly dwindled away until she looked like a skeleton. The pain and suffering her children felt was unbearable and unfair. They will not be able to have their mom around when they graduate high school, college, get married or have children. It has been traumatizing for her husband who loved her dearly. The kids have had many struggles since their mom died, especially the youngest child who has been in and out of a lot of trouble.

The slides should have been read properly. The lab tech should have been better supervised by the lead pathologist. The lab techs in that facility should not have been under pressure to read over fifty slides a day. A better system should have been in place. This young mom should be alive today. This case was heartbreaking for me. I could literally feel her pain up until the last day of her life, including the sadness she felt for her children. "

Anna, Paralegal

Anna was at risk for Vicarious Trauma because of her intense and ongoing professional involvement with the husband and children of the victim. Her professional involvement began to impose a personal bias because, from Anna's point of view, this was a traumatic event that could certainly have happened to her. Additionally, she had to control her empathic response, taxing her brain's ability to automatically resolve what would have been a grievous but normalizing and balanced response.

When we are deeply distressed or just can't shake a client's story, we are probably having difficulty negotiating the biochemical stress response or we may have become less and less effective at doing so (Compassion Fatigue). We may even be surprised at what might trigger the stress response from that story: an item in a magazine, an image we see out of the corner of our eye, a character in a story we are reading. We are struggling in our own ability to calm our sympathetic nervous system. *Helping* professionals will find their inner experience of self, others, and their Higher Power transformed in ways that parallel the experience of the trauma survivor. In other words, symptoms of Vicarious Trauma closely parallel symptoms of Post Traumatic Stress Disorder.

Here are some warning signs of Vicarious Trauma:

- Emotional exhaustion: the emotional overextension of contact with others that results in draining your energy. Emotional exhaustion includes feelings of apathy, entrapment, dissatisfaction, hopelessness, helplessness, nervousness, irritability, discouragement and emptiness.
- Depersonalization: an unfeeling and hardened response to others.
- Reduced personal accomplishment: a decreased sense of professionalism or achievement in your work with others.
- Somatization: this includes change in appetite, gastrointestinal disturbance, anger, low self-esteem, self-doubt, impaired judgment and reasoning.

The symptoms of Vicarious Trauma run parallel with Post Traumatic Stress Disorder and include:

- distressing emotions;
- hyperarousal;
- disruptions in the cognitive schema of *helper* identity, memory, and belief system;
- intrusive imagery, such as nightmares or recurring visualizations;
- emotional numbing;
- inability to tolerate strong emotions or hypersensitivity to emotionally charged stimulations, such as movies or television;
- feeling fearful or overly concerned for family members;
- dissociation;
- somatization in which psychological symptoms present as physical ailments and physical illness;
- isolation and diminished capacity to enjoy significant activities; and
- feelings of incompetence (Saakvitne & Pearlman, 1996).

Let us introduce you to a marriage and family therapist named Marilyn who came to treatment because she was suffering from a sleep disorder and no longer wanted to take medication in order to get a night's rest. When asked to journal what she thought about while lying awake, she wrote the following:

> *"As I'm lying here tonight, I've decided that this is as good a time as any to journal for you what goes on in my mind as I am still awake at one in the morn-*

ing when I have clients tomorrow from 8AM to 7PM, straight through, with no break. I think about a client who came to me with a horrific story. I am working with a mother whose daughter was found dead in her apartment in Manhattan. The girl had been brutalized, raped and strangled. When she had to go and identify her daughter, the mother sobbed, stating that her daughter was unrecognizable. She was only eighteen years old, in her first year of school. At home, she had a six-year-old who needed to understand what happened to her sister. The mother, in her grief, wants to relate the sordid details and I am struggling with my own personal judgments about her desire to do this.

Marilyn, Marriage and Family Therapist

This therapist was intensely struggling with Vicarious Trauma that was complicated by an historical event in her own life. When Marilyn was 10 years old, her 16-year-old sister was beaten to death by a gang in the inner city of Detroit where she lived at the time with her family. The therapist had a three-dimensional challenge: 1) addressing the client's Post Traumatic Stress Disorder and grief; 2) addressing the client's parental responsibility to protect her 6-year-old child; and, 3) to stay in check of her own intense emotional and physiological reactions to the trauma of the client and the endangerment of the child. And she wondered why she couldn't sleep? She got stuck in the unresolved neurocircuitry of controlled empathy, which can feel like obsessive thoughts that kept her awake night after night.

Controlled empathy is the capacity to efficiently and accurately monitor another's state of being and it is the specific channel through which Vicarious Trauma occurs. It is precisely in the empathic witnessing of the client's experience that our heroes risk fundamentally and permanently having their world view altered. Empathic capacity is the professional's aptitude for controlled empathy and it varies among *helping* professionals.

Overuse of controlled empathy can spawn an existential crisis called the Abyss. The Abyss is the intense emotional cauldron of a deregulated affective state expressed in altered patterns of attachment, relationship, experience of horror, abandonment by humanity and spiritual challenge of meaning (International Trauma Consultants, 2006). A person in this state has little or no awareness or control over his or her emotions, internally or externally. Furthermore, the Abyss becomes profoundly disturbing to professionals who believe that their training renders them invulnerable to extreme emotional stress. The *helper* may not be conscious that anything is even happening or may go into a form of denial, based in shame that something like Vicarious Trauma could happen to him or her at all.

Our heroes frequently work with clients who have suffered Post Traumatic Stress Disorder. This type of client presents stories we hear routinely and these stories have an effect on us. In the performance of their duties, our heroes may participate in any of four types of witnessing experiences. These experiences directly impact *helpers* and clients alike, but because of the central role *helpers* may play in clients' lives, the long-term effects can also ripple outward. If *helping* professionals are not able to manage their witnessing experiences effectively, harmful consequences may extend to personal relationships, colleagues and the community at large.

The following table is taken from an article in Counselor Magazine (2004), *Common Shock: Witnessing Violence in Clients' Lives.*

	AWARE	UNAWARE
EMPOWERED	Effective and Competent Position. 1	Misguided, Possible Malpractice Position. 2
DISEMPOWERED	Ineffectual And Stressed Position. 3	Abandoning, Possible Malpractice Position. 4

Allow us to explain. The first witnessing position is Stage One: empowered and aware. The *helper* is someone who feels effective and competent to address the situation at hand, who is not dissociating from or avoiding the trauma context, who is hearing the story with controlled empathy and not finding herself or himself in an elicited trauma response. This is a win-win situation for all concerned. Following is a submission from a lawyer who was able to maintain a Stage One (empowered and aware) position with his client:

"I had a case in which a family retained my services for a medical malpractice incident that really hit close to home. The mother of the family had a minor back problem for which she elected to have surgery. The surgery was successful and the mother seemed to be enjoying an uneventful recovery initially. On the

third day after the surgery, one of her children came for a visit and noticed that her mother's color was ashen and upon feeling mother's forehead, noticed that mother was feverish. Her mother complained of a sharp pain on her lower left side. The child quickly reported this to the nursing staff and was assured the doctor would be in to check on her mother sometime that morning. The child left to go to work and assured her mother she would return later that day. When she returned her mother's fever was further elevated, she was semi-conscious and unable to communicate effectively. The child went back to the nurses' station and received a report that the doctor had seen the mother earlier in the day and had ordered antibiotics to be administered intravenously. Even though the daughter was very upset, she went home that evening, slept fitfully, and awoke early and returned to the hospital to be with her mother. When she got there, the bed was empty. Her mother had died in the course of the night and no one had called her or the family to let them know. I handled this case for the family, but it was very difficult for me. My own mother had died shortly after bypass surgery five years earlier. I had to keep my own history and personal pain out of the conference room and out of my negotiations. I actually consulted with the therapist that I worked with when my mother died to ensure that I remained objective and untouched by my own trauma response. I won, you know. They gave the woman the wrong antibiotic – she was septic and they missed it. The clients won a huge award, but sadly, lost their mother."

Martin, Lawyer

The second stage witnessing position is Stage Two: empowered and unaware. It occurs when *helpers* respond as if they are aware but not consciously checking in with the severity, significance or impact of what the client's story is telling them. In these situations, *helpers* are not truly connecting with the reality of the *trauma content* and how it related to their client. This may ultimately be seen as a professional abandonment and could be viewed as a form of malpractice. *Helpers* are *responding* as if they know what they are doing and may find themselves ineffective at best, guilty of passive behavior toward their client and of possible malpractice at worst. In reality, the *helpers* are not effectively treating their clients – they are minimizing the client story because of their own Vicarious Trauma. The *helpers'* personal symptoms of Vicarious Trauma include numbing out or dissociating from the *trauma content* narrative. This process has also been called Collusive Resistance in which *helpers* unconsciously or consciously join their clients in avoiding a painful and traumatic experience (Fox and Carey, 1999)

The following is a Stage Two story from a mediator:

> *"A husband and wife were going through a divorce with my help. I am a law-yer/ mediator. On numerous occasions during our meetings the wife attempted to describe to me, in the presence of her husband, detailed and graphic accounts of conflictual interactions between she and her husband and between her husband and their two small children. She described verbally violent episodes that she perceived as very traumatizing to herself and her children. She related intimidating, demeaning and threatening conversations that the husband vehemently denied. The husband alleged that the wife was exaggerating and that she was simply trying to discredit him to me. Her rationale, he explained, was to increase her parenting time and cause him to have additional child support to pay. There were never any police reports filed and I had no other collateral information to support the wife's narratives. The wife eventually stopped relating her stories and agreed to move forward with the mediation. In my assessment of the situation, the husband presented as calm, rationale, logical and cooperative. The husband never had a bad word to say about the wife. In fact, he spoke very highly of her parenting skills and her relationship with the children. He denied any and all allegations presented by the wife, citing his children's desire to spend time with him as their little league coach and active participant in their lives. Divorcing is a very stressful situation. Although I saw impatience on the part of the father at times, I assumed it was appropriate behavior based on the stress level of the couple going through this divorce. My role was to facilitate a negotiated agreement, a win-win solution for this couple, and so we proceeded with mediation and reached agreement over the course of several meetings. One day, after the final agreement had been reached, the husband contacted me by cell phone to discuss changing a certain phrase in the parenting agreement. Once our conversation had concluded, the husband thought the phone call was disconnected. However, he failed to disconnect from the call and I overheard his communications with the children while he continued driving with them in the car. These communications were demeaning, threatening, abusive and violent, containing accusations and name-calling about the mother. The children were crying and begging him to stop. I was horrified that I had so misjudged the situation. At this point, the agreement was finished and no further meetings were scheduled, with the exception of having the clients come in to sign the document. I believed my job was done. The following week, the couple came to sign the documents at my office. Once finished, the wife left first, while the husband used the rest room, or so I thought. She got into the elevator, he jammed his hand between the elevator doors before they closed, and*

forced his way in. He stabbed her once in the chest and several times in other parts of her body. She died later at our local hospital."

Fred, Lawyer/Mediator

There was nothing lacking in Fred professionally. He was well-trained but had become numbed due to Vicarious Trauma. Because of his unrecognized Vicarious Trauma, he failed to intervene on behalf of his female client. Unfortunately, after years of hearing similar stories Fred had become desensitized or numbed when hearing narratives regarding domestic abuse. His lack of awareness precipitated poor professional judgment and ultimately cost the life of one of his clients. Now Fred has to deal with the ongoing grief of thinking about two children who have lost both their parents to something much worse than divorce. Fred still worries to this day about professional and civil repercussions in his future cases.

The next witness position is Stage Three: aware and disempowered. It is found when professionals are highly conscious of what needs to be done and are aware of the situation but feel powerless to provide any viable help. This is one of the most traumatizing witnessing positions for *helpers* to face. *Helpers* who are keenly aware of the client's situation but feel helpless to do anything about it will be of little or no use to their clients. They will also be highly stressed by their work. This situation places *helpers* in the role of little more than a bystander. The following heart-wrenching story was told by a hospital based social worker:

"I work at a children's hospital with transplant cases. In most cases, patients die before we can get them the organs they so desperately need. One case that plays over and over in my mind is a case of a seven-year-old boy who had been waiting for three months for a kidney. His health was declining fast. He was brought in shortly before Christmas in a physiological crisis. Dialysis was no longer effective and his system was crashing. His doctor was concerned that he would not survive the weekend. For 48 hours I lived on the telephone in my office. I called every hospital, every ER, every social service agency, every transplant team, desperate to find a warm body to talk to. I so wanted to save this little boy's life. With each voicemail I left and each menu I had to navigate, I felt more and more desperate. I didn't want to have to tell his parents I failed. But I did, and he died. Never before in my job had I operated in a scenario where I was so powerless. For months, I felt directly responsible for his death.

After a year of therapy, I am finally coming to terms with the failure of our medical system. I no longer blame myself, but I sure am bitter."

Grace, Licensed Clinical Social Worker

Grace suffered with a very distressing witnessing position. Our heroes are frequently haunted by events in which they were extremely conscious of what needed to be done but felt powerless or lacking in any form of support to provide it.

The final witnessing position is Stage Four: unaware and disempowered. In this stage, *helping* professionals find themselves passive in relationship to the urgent needs of their clients and they ultimately abandon their clients because of this ignorance and lack of awareness. The professionals' own Vicarious Trauma has overridden both their professional skills and personal awareness so that the *helpers* are physically present, but emotionally and professionally absent. The following is an account of a Stage Four story provided by a psychologist:

"I am a trauma survivor myself and have worked for over 20 years with survivors of sexual abuse in my practice. As a child, my parents crossed sexual boundaries with me but not with malicious intent. I had done forgiveness work with my therapist several years before this case walked through my door and I believed that I had healed from my own personal trauma. The client shared with me a history that was brimming with many levels of domestic violence. Her father, an alcoholic and drug addict, terrorized and assaulted every member of her family. When the client was three years old, she remembered her father touched her inappropriately as he gave her a bath. This sexual abuse intensified over time so that by age eight, he was forcing her older brother to participate in the abuse while her father looked on. When I heard the story, I mistakenly assessed that the client would overcome this heinous form of abuse as I had survived mine. Wrong! The client carried far more disturbance than I tuned into in the course of our work together. While I utilized certain therapeutic processes that were appropriate for this type of client, it certainly was not enough for someone who presented with this type of childhood trauma. In retrospect, the client needed to be under the ongoing care of a psychiatrist for medication evaluation, she needed to seek out and become a member of an adult survivor of childhood sexual abuse support group, and she needed to be

treated by a more experienced therapist who specialized in this type of sexual violence. Eventually the client's symptoms became worse and she developed hallucinations and paranoia. I referred her for a more intensive program of treatment. I probably needed to do that after our first consultation, but I really thought I had my finger on the pulse of her problem. I think about her often and wish I had acted sooner. While I don't think I did the patient any direct harm, I don't believe I did her much good."

Bethany, Psychologist

Bethany had to take a close look at how Vicarious Trauma had desensitized her response to sexual assault clients and how her own personal treatment and her belief about other people's treatment impacted her assessment skills in this case. She believed that if she could survive her childhood trauma and function at a high level, so could anyone else. Her judgment was impaired, her ability to assess the needs of her client was impaired, and her treatment lacked the dimension that the client deserved to receive. The phenomenon of countertransference, which played a significant role in this case, will be examined more closely in Chapter 6.

Vicarious Trauma may cause permanent changes in the *helper's* world view. The world begins to be perceived as a dark place where no one is emotionally safe. The pathway to the spiritual perspective is broken. Helping professionals may suffer compromised basic needs. Safety, trust, esteem, intimacy and control needs are adversely affected in those suffering with Vicarious Trauma (Saakvitne & Pearlman, 1996). One such extreme example is George, a pastor of a large congregation in the South:

"I serve a large congregation in the deep South. I am revered and thought of as a man of kindness, great wisdom and vision. Congregants approach me on a daily basis for advice, wisdom, forgiveness and hope for the future. I rarely have a day that I am not bombarded with needy people. The classic line I hear is, 'Pastor George, can I just have a moment of your time?' Even when I attend social events, someone needs to unload on me. When I first took on this congregation, I encouraged my congregants to reach out for my help. Sometimes you have to be careful what you pray for! Over the years, I found myself in a deepening spiritual crisis. It is really hard to preach the word of God when you are in conflict about whether He's really listening. I am so depressed about the person I have become. When I was a student in seminary, I was so faithful about the protection offered in a relationship with God. Today I am not the same person. How could God abandon all his children through the atrocities

of this world? How do I explain his work to my congregation when I've lost my faith? I am worried because sooner or later they will notice this change in me. They are not stupid. I have become sullen and less approachable. I have less patience, and I fear I am failing my congregation and myself. I am not a perfect person and I am certainly a disappointment to God and my congregation. I live with this negativity everyday and have no one to talk to. Thankfully, I am anonymous in this writing or my shame would envelop me..."

Pastor George

Pastor George is a painful example of a *helper* who has suffered an inner transformation of his own identity, due to bearing witness to domestic violence, child abuse, death, rape and other traumatizing events. He never realized that it is absolutely acceptable to have his own personal experience of feeling outraged, horrified, shocked saddened or vulnerable to attack. His shame over being human prevented him from seeking his own path of recovery which would have helped him to remember that his normal human reactions need not sever him from his faith. Sadly, he left the church and suffered criticism from the congregation for abandoning them. On a more positive note, he sought counseling for his Vicarious Trauma, reconnected with his spiritual self and is considering returning to a new congregation.

CHAPTER SIX

Countertransference and the Wounded Hero

When a professional is helping someone, there is a conscious and an unconscious part of the *helping* relationship. The conscious part of a *helping* relationship is the overt activity that goes on between the client and the *helper*. When someone comes for help, the *helper* simply gives that help in whatever way is appropriate for his or her designated profession, i.e., lawyer, doctor, therapist, etc. An unconscious relationship dimension, called countertransference, affects every *helping* professional. Countertransference is the displacement of *helper* emotion onto the client or as it is more generally identified the heroes emotional involvement in the *helping* interaction (Earley, 2006).

This unconscious part can get away from us and if left unaddressed can cause a lot of pain for both the client and the *helper*. At some level every person we meet in our work reminds us of someone who impacted us at an earlier time in our own human development. Stored memories can become triggered and the feeling states connected to those memories rise to the consciousness. Vicarious Trauma makes it exceedingly difficult to tune in to that second dimension of the *helping* relationship because Vicarious Trauma sufferers may be numbed, dissociated, distracted or in denial of those unconscious parts of their own lives. While this countertransference phenomenon is considered a normal psychological process, it is important for *helpers* to have an awareness of it when it is happening so that they might help their clients with integrity and accountability.

The other aspect of Vicarious Trauma we need to address when discussing countertransference is the neurocircuitry behind it that stimulates hippocampal activity. The hippocampus is considered to be the relay station regarding the storage of memories. If a *helper* is an adult survivor of childhood trauma, his or her own traumatic memories may be triggered, throwing the *helper* into an intense personal crisis (Wilson & Lindy. 1999). *Helpers* need to recognize their own internal reactivity and seek appropriate counsel and consultation to address this existential upset. Otherwise, it compromises their ability to address the issues of the client. Even worse, *helpers* are now at risk to act in or act out around their own painful historical triggers.

In cases where *helpers* are suffering from Vicarious Trauma, they may be unaware of their own countertransference issues because they are either consciously avoiding or unconsciously dissociating from the event. The danger this presents is that of *helpers* placing themselves in an incapable position; if they are unaware of their own personal reactions, *helpers* will be jaded in the responses hey provide and the clients' best interests cannot be served (Wilson & Lindy, 2004).

As stated previously, at least 53% of *helping* professionals report themselves to be trauma survivors. That percentage is most likely understated because many *helpers* are shamed to embrace, much less report, their own trauma history. Unfortunately, this type of denial or repression leaves *helpers* at risk to experience a countertransference phenomenon.

One particular study surveyed over 500 clinicians in which more than 32% reported childhood sexual abuse histories (Pearlman & Mac Ian, 1995). Sexually abused therapists are more likely to report countertransference issues, especially boundary issues, than non-abused therapists. Successful boundary negotiation by a therapist involves efficient recognition of the emptiness and terror that a perceived threat to attachment can produce. The most common error in countertransference management with Vicarious Trauma victims is a sudden and unexplained change in boundary rules. For example, consider the following case example submitted by Cherisse, a therapist who was an adult survivor of childhood abuse.

> *"This may sound like a small incident, but I found myself highly agitated when this situation would come up. I worked with a client named Louise who was an adult child of an alcoholic. She came to counseling to heal from being raised by a physically violent alcoholic mother. When Louise's mother would drink, she would become extremely violent and physically assault Louise. Her physical assaults usually included banging her head against the wall or on a countertop. Louise's mother directed every aspect of her life. She never learned to function independently. She moved from life with an intrusive mother into a marriage with a tyrannical husband. Louise really had difficulty acknowledging her legitimate anger toward her mother and used pity as a substitute. Anger was a difficult emotion for Louise to negotiate and at a young age, she got into passive aggressive expressions of her angry feelings. This was recreated in the therapeutic relationship by Louise running chronically late for our meetings. What I was*

unaware of was that I was not protecting my own boundaries, something that has always been a challenge as a result of my own trauma history. Louise would be 15 minutes late for her appointment, the session would run 10 minutes over and I would feel angry that I was back-peddling for the rest of my day with my subsequent appointments. One particular day, Louise showed up at 9:20 for her 9 a.m. appointment. Since her appointment should have been completed at 9:50, on this day, I closed the session at exactly that time. Louise looked at her watch and challenged me that she did not have enough counseling time. I shared with her my interpretation of her chronic lateness and boundary issues exemplified by her misuse of time. I realized through my anger at her that I was experiencing a countertransference phenomenon. I had allowed the client to intrude upon my boundaries of time management and this elicited an upset that had its roots in a much earlier time in my life. Luckily, I was conscious enough to notice the countertransference, identify it, and process it with the client as a catalyst for her own self-awareness and growth. The client initially appeared irritated at my boundary setting because it was a change from what she had grown accustomed to; however, after considering my explanation she seemed calmer as she left the session. My client still runs at least 15 minutes late for her sessions, but now, we end promptly at 10 minutes to the hour."

Cherisse, Licensed Professional Counselor

Fortunately, Cherisse was in touch with her own normal countertransference triggers, able to recognize her anger, process it internally, and label it as a boundary intrusion. She managed her own historical arousal of anger in a responsible and productive way through which the client gained some useful awareness for how she covertly expresses her own anger. At the time of this writing, the client's behavior had not yet changed and she was still running chronically late. However, the client was able to understand, through the productive conversation shared with Cherisse, that her tardy behavior impacted others. The client also began to understand the importance of developing emotional maturity so that she might parent herself through effective time management.

Another example of countertransference is illustrated in a story where a family lawyer was stressing to his female client the importance of achieving A's in her college courses because that client reminded him of his daughter who was living singly and trying to move forward in an independent lifestyle. His anxieties about his own daughter created a pathway to this countertransference with his client. The lawyer in this example is transferring his unconscious paternal feelings to his client.

Countertransference is defined in opposition to transference in which a client in a *helping* relationship begins to transfer feelings (whether positive or negative) onto the professional. For example, a person in therapy may begin to look at the therapist as if the therapist were the patient's mother, transferring his or her feelings for the real mother to the therapist. While this is considered a positive sign in psychoanalytical therapy, showing that the patient is making progress, it also presents an emotional stressor for the therapist. *Helpers* who have not had counseling training may not recognize this transference and may act on it in a negative way. Developing insight and becoming educated about these transference/countertransference phenomena is essential if you are working in the *helping* professions.

Literature suggests that countertransference has the potential to be present in any *helping* relationship. The research states that it is often one of the biggest challenges for new *helpers* to overcome and while there is no way to totally overcome the problem of countertransference (since as humans we all form opinions of others), learning to not let countertransference affect a *helping* relationship is key. Countertransference can also be seen as a useful phenomenon for *helpers* because it can allow them to gain insight into the kinds of emotions and reactions the client often tends to induce in others. In this way, countertransference is a welcomed phenomenon that can provide invaluable insight to the *helping* relationship. (Kennedy, 1993)

According to Jay Earley (2006), the following are transference and countertransference patterns that any *helper* needs to be aware of. In order to reduce the potential for Vicarious Trauma, *helpers* need to be well informed and aware of their own countertransference issues and responses so that they can protect themselves from accumulating upsetting feeling states that begin to take their toll. Over time, the occupational hazards inherent in the *helping* professions will wreak havoc on the *helpers'* health. It is happening every day, even though it is not visible or palpable. Awareness is your first line of defense.

NEEDY PATTERN	**Transference**	Sees therapist as nurturing mother; dependent.
		Sees therapist as non-nurturing mother; hurt; angry.
	Countertransference	Overly involved in caring for client.
		Repulsed by client's needs.

NEED-DENYING PATTERN	Transference	Denies need for nurturing or help from therapist.
	Countertransference	Happy that client doesn't need anything.
INSECURE PATTERN	Transference	Afraid therapist is judgmental of her or doesn't like her.
	Countertransference	Overly involved in reassuring client. Repulsed by client's insecurities.
ISOLATED PATTERN	Transference	Avoidance of personal/emotional relationship with therapist or denial of it.
	Countertransference	Treating relationship as if it were only instrumental. Moving too quickly to connect with the client.
COMPLIANT PATTERN	Transference	Pretends that everything the therapist does works.
	Countertransference	Believes the client's compliance.
DEFIANT PATTERN	Transference	Refuses to cooperate with much of the therapy. Fights with therapist and criticizes her approach.
	Countertransference	Feels ineffective and incompetent. Feels hurt by criticisms. Becomes frustrated with client. Gets into arguments and power struggles with client.
PASSIVE-AGGRESSIVE PATTERN	Transference	Experiences the therapist as pressuring her to perform. Consciously wants to please the therapist, but fails to do therapy correctly, or if she does, fails to progress in life or denies progress. Unconsciously, this is an expression of anger at the therapist and an attempt to defeat the therapist, who she experiences as attempting to control her and change her.
	Countertransference	Becomes frustrated with the client for failing. Feels ineffective and incompetent.
CONTROLLING PATTERN	Transference	Refuses to allow therapist to do much. Must be in control of the therapy.
	Countertransference	Gets into a power struggle with the client.

VICTIM PATTERN	Transference	Complains to therapist about his misery in unconscious attempt to get therapist to do it for him.
		Blames therapist for his problems for same unconscious reason.
	Countertransference	Fails to see victim stance and keeps trying to reassure and encourage client.
		Becomes angry and frustrated with client.
CO-DEPENDENT PATTERN	Transference	Tries to take care of therapist.
		Picks up on clues of therapist's pain or life struggles and engages therapist in talking about them.
		Notices therapist's insecurities and assuages them.
	Countertransference	Allows client to take care of him.
SUSPICIOUS PATTERN	Transference	Suspects that the therapist harbors negative feelings toward him that are hidden or that the therapist will at some point turn on him or abandon him. Doesn't trust positive things he sees.
	Countertransference	Becomes annoyed at client for lack of trust and hides this from client, thereby making client's fears come true. Pressures client to trust prematurely.
AGGRESSIVE PATTERN	Transference	Periodically becomes enraged at therapist over a certain behavior of situation that develops.
		Criticizes the therapist's handling of the therapy.
	Countertransference	Becomes frightened of client's anger and tries to avoid triggering it, leading to non-therapeutic behavior.
		Becomes angry at client and shows it directly or covertly. Feels hurt by criticism, leading to feelings of incompetence.
		Argues with client about content of criticisms.

SELF-JUDGING PATTERN	Transference	Constantly blames himself for poor performance in therapy and life. Often expects therapist to feel the same way.
	Countertransference	Tries to reassure client without directly working n the inner critic. Becomes annoyed with client for constant self-judgment, thereby contributing to it.
CHARMING PATTERN	Transference	Entertains the therapist with fascinating stories. Engages the therapist's sexual interest. Charms the therapist.
	Countertransference	Becomes more interested in the client's charm (in whichever form) than in engaging in therapy.
BRITTLE FORM OF DEFENSIVE PATTERN	Transference	Becomes deeply hurt by challenges from the therapist (or things perceived that way) and reacts with brittle defenses.
	Countertransference	Tries to reassure the client without dealing with underlying issues. Keeps going with the challenge. Becomes frustrated that client can't deal with any challenges.
PRIDEFUL PATTERN	Transference	Expects therapist to appreciate or admire him. Acts superior and demeaning toward therapist.
	Countertransference	Therapist admires client or gives appreciation, thinking client needs support. Therapist becomes angry at client for grandiosity or condescension and challenges him in an unsupportive way.
ENTITLED PATTERN	Transference	Client expects special favors from therapist around money, time, etc. Client expects therapist to give him exactly what he wants. In making these demands, the client completely disregards any needs or limits the therapist might have.
	Countertransference	Therapist gives in to client's demands. Therapist becomes angry at client's demands and at therapists needs being ignored.

Here is one testimonial and exceptional explanation from the viewpoint of a psychiatrist who did evaluations for the judicial system. Her story is posted online under the name "Dr. Sanity" [drsanity.blogspot.com].

> *"Some years ago I used to moonlight and perform psychiatric evaluations for the prosecutors and public defenders in the county where I lived. Personality disorders have always been an interest of mine, and you can find many examples in the jails and prisons.*
>
> *One particular case stands out in my mind. I was asked by the public defender to evaluate a young man who was accused of murdering his girlfriend. The man was adamant that he was innocent and his lawyer wanted to believe him, but something didn't seem quite right to him, so he decided to ask me for my psychiatric opinion of his client and evaluate the possibility that there might be a psychiatric defense.*
>
> *Steve was, to all intents and purposes, a model citizen in many ways. He held a responsible job; had no prior legal problems. He had been going with his girlfriend for about 3 months when her body was found in a wooded area--not too far from the apartment complex where he lived. Naturally, he was the prime suspect in her murder (she was strangled). There was also some physical evidence present that linked him to her death, but he insisted that she had left his apartment earlier that morning to go to work after spending the night with him and he had not seen her after that.*
>
> *When I met with him, I experienced what we used to call in medical school a "Positive Gorney Sign"--meaning that the hair on the back of my neck stood on end. It is a "gut feeling" that something very strange is going on--something that may not be readily obvious to a casual observer, or on first inspection.*
>
> *In my career, I have learned to respect such feelings. It almost always means that I need to look more closely at a patient and pay more attention to what they are saying or doing that might be stimulating my instinctive emotional response.*
>
> *Occasionally, I find no corroborating evidence in their behavior for such feelings, and in those cases I simply file the emotional data away and make a conscious decision not to act on it for the time being. Sometimes I find negative*

evidence that contradicts my primal emotional response. Both situations are cues to me that I must try to figure out what it was that triggered my emotion, and the first step is to look within myself for an explanation. Does the patient remind me of someone I have ambivalent feelings about? Am I upset at something going on in my life? Am I having a bad day? Because it is important to realize that gut feelings can be communicating false data about others, but correct data about one's self.

A person's visceral response to another individual is usually based on mostly unconscious factors that are in play in the responder's life. To make an assessment of the gut feeling's appropriateness, the contents of the unconscious must be explored and brought to the conscious level and considered. Those unconscious internal conflicts can easily mask the inappropriate aspects of the feelings, making them worthless as a means of understanding the external world.

Taking this kind of action as a method of checking and understanding one's own feelings is a process called "insight" or "self-awareness". Some people do this quite naturally and honestly. Some learn in therapy or when they are in crisis. But if insight is absent then one's feelings have the potential to do great harm --both to one's self and to others.

Some unconscious factors, or psychological defenses, that can make one's feelings untrustworthy are: 1) the person you are responding to has become symbolic of someone else in your life (displacement, fantasy, or perhaps distortion); 2) focusing on one particular aspect of a person, you ignore other, more objective data that are available to you about the person (denial); 3) you place your own unacceptable feelings onto the other person--e.g., I'm not an angry person, -- he's an angry person! (projection or full-blown paranoia).

The truth is that there are countless ways that unconscious processes within ourselves can distort our responses to others and to reality itself. Growing up and attaining maturity requires that we take a moment to consider such factors playing a role in our emotions before we act on those emotions. If we come to know ourselves and understand our own weaknesses, vulnerabilities, limitations and secrets; then our emotional responses to people or to the world can be very valuable tools to help interpret the world. But they are only tools, and if not used wisely, they can do more harm than good. Feelings cannot be used in a court of law--for good reason. And they are not ultimate truth in the court of reality, either.

As I have gained experience in psychiatry, more often than not, when I trust such feelings and proceed to analyze what is bothering me about the situation, I discover a wealth of information that would have otherwise remained hidden. Sometimes that "wealth of information" is only about me; but even in that case, I learn something new --frequently something insightful that I didn't want to know--about myself.

For example, I recently became aware that I was extremely annoyed and inappropriately angry at a 70 year-old woman, who was not getting better in treatment because she refused to acknowledge that she had a severe drinking problem.

My anger at this sad, elderly lady was completely out of proportion to the situation-- after all, I have numerous patients that do exactly the same thing, and their behavior does not typically bring out such intense feelings in me.

"Why doesn't she tell herself the truth?" I thought. Then I realized that this thought was what I used to verbalize with some anguish to my own mother--who died of her alcoholism at age 72; refusing all my entreaties to get help and treatment. My entire interaction with this elderly patient was all about my own unresolved anger and grief toward my mother's death and not about the patient at all. Once I appreciated that I had to deal with my issues separately and not force my patient into a role she hadn't asked for, I could respond to her for who she really was; and maybe even help her. The reality was that she wasn't my mother, though my mind had made her so.

In psychiatry, we refer to feelings like those that I projected onto my patient as "Countertransference". We are generally aware that our own feelings are not always a reliable tool for interpreting reality. In fact, they may misdirect us or even completely interfere with our attempts to help another person.

What a person feels in a particular situation is also an incontrovertible fact; but it may or may not reveal any real information about the situation--and only reveal information about the person who is experiencing the feeling. To remember that this is the rule, rather than the exception about feelings, all we need do is to observe the chaotic lives of most of our patients, where thinking is almost always subsumed by emotion.

With all those caveats, it is still true that using one's own feelings as a clinical barometer can at times be very helpful. I am aware, for example, that I have a very reliable emotional reaction to those patients with borderline/narcissistic/antisocial personalities. To put it simply, I find myself feeling amused and entertained by patients with these personality traits.

This is in stark contrast to most of my colleagues, who generally come to feel extremely frustrated and angry at such patients. My emotional response is probably the reason why I don't get "burned out" professionally in dealing with these difficult patients, while many of my colleagues run like hell from them. So, when I am evaluating a person for the first time, and I find that I am responding in an amused fashion or if I have a feeling that I am being lied to or manipulated--or even if I sense that there is something I can't quite put my finger on-- these emotional data points/reactions can add to the other evidence I collect in order to make specific diagnoses.

In contrast, when dealing with a depressed and passive patient, I frequently find myself responding to their plight with feelings of frustration and often experience a transient fantasy of wanting to shake the person and say, "this is your LIFE! Why are you wasting it?"

Clearly, I try to reign in this response since it is counterproductive and not particularly useful for my patient in their current state of emotional distress. But it can confirm the diagnosis of depression, if I had any doubt about it.

Now, back to Steve. My reaction to him was very revealing. Besides the sign I mentioned above, I found myself amused at his attempts to manipulate my response to him and began to suspect that there was a serious personality disorder behind the civilized facade that he presented. Although I felt he was trying a little too hard to convince me of his bona fides, I was impressed when he told me he had received a community award for rescuing a woman the year before.

He remained adamant about his innocence. I found that I didn't believe him, despite his obvious passionate protestations of innocence. I began to understand the unease that my lawyer friend was having about the case, but after almost 2 hours of talking to Steve, I had no other data except for my gut feeling that he wasn't telling me the truth; and my suspicion that I was dealing with someone with strong psychopathological personality traits at the least and a full-blown antisocial personality at the other extreme.

If my feelings had been the sole data point, I would have determinedly ignored them. To confirm my unease, I would have to search for some objective data to support my unease about Steve.

So I asked for the hundreds of pages of documents that are generated from a criminal investigation. These are the pages and pages of notes from the first policemen on the scene and the interviews of all the people connected with the case. Eventually I read the detective's notes from the first interview with Steve at the beginning of the case, before he became the prime suspect.

Interestingly, Steve apparently knew the detective who had interviewed him in this murder case, from a previous interaction with him almost a year ago. In our interview, I remembered that Steve had mentioned his positive feelings about the detective from their previous encounter, and his optimism that evidence would be found exonerating him. Even more interestingly, this previous interaction with the detective was in connection to the event Steve briefly mentioned to me about earning a community award.

My gut feeling returned even stronger. THIS IS IMPORTANT! It was the message it transmitted to me. I immediately obtained records about the incident of one year ago, and here is the information as I pieced it together.

A year earlier, a woman jogger had been shot by a sniper. This crime had taken place fairly close to the apartment building that Steve had lived in at the time, near a park. Steve reportedly had also been jogging, heard the shot, and saw the woman fall. He immediately ran to her aid, calling 911 and then administering CPR and keeping the woman alive until help came. Sadly, the woman jogger later died of her wound in the hospital. But Steve was honored with a "Good Samaritan" award from the city. The police detective who interviewed him for that murder case was the same one that took his statement a year later in the murder of his girlfriend.

Do you begin to see where this gut feeling was taking me? This could most certainly be an amazing coincidence, but my gut feeling was telling me it wasn't a coincidence at all. On the contrary, my instinct--my feeling--told me this was no coincidence.

The police had not yet made the connection between the two cases (I have no doubt that they eventually would have, without my help) I called the detective and asked him if he remembered Steve. He did not. When I prompted him about the other case, there was a short silence, then a faint gasp.

That murder had never been solved. The detective assured me he would look into it; and sure enough, a few weeks later, he called me to report that they had found the sniper's gun for the previous crime in a locker at Steve's workplace.

Steve's public defender had to fire me, since --not only could I not help his current case, but I had implicated his client in another murder. If only Steve had not needed to tell me about his "community award" -- a statement which didn't feel right in the context of our interview; then I probably would never have made the connection. But Steve provided the connection, and my emotional reaction to Steve motivated me to follow through and Steve's civilized cover was blown. He was eventually convicted of the woman jogger's murder as well as the strangulation of his girlfriend (which was motivated by her telling him she was pregnant). Police were actively looking into several other unsolved murders of young women in that area of the city to see if there could be any connection to Steve.

So, why am I telling this story? Because I believe that feelings are an extremely important resource all people have at their disposal for understanding the world around us. In some situations, the only thing we have we have to help us make decisions are our feelings. This is not the ideal, but sometimes it can suffice.

Humans are both feeling and thinking beings. If we ignore our feelings we have psychologically blinded ourselves to important information about the world; and if we ignore our mind and our reason, we have done the same thing. If we do not use both faculties together, we do not see the whole inner and outer world of reality.

The unquestioning reliance on one's feelings as the be-all and end-all of perceiving reality has some MAJOR, MAJOR snags associated with it. It leads to cha-

otic, dysfunctional relationships, instability, histrionic and impulsive behavior, and a lack of concern for the needs and feelings of other people.

It has been my experience that many people have a sort of primitive, child-like reverence for whatever they feel. That's all they know and all they need to know, seemingly. They never bother to try to understand why they feel the way they do; or even to objectively understand the source feelings. Indeed, it isn't always necessary to do so, but for many, living has become a matter of, 'I feel, therefore I am.'

Well, I am here to tell you that this is the motto of the Steves of the world--who function exclusively on the basis of their feelings--and who have no room or inclination to bother with anybody else's feelings or needs. Why the Steve's of the world are all wrapped up in themselves and their feelings, and why--despite their verbalizations to the contrary, they are truly incapable of the empathy with other people.

Empathy, or the ability to feel what others are feeling, is actually a healthy form of psychological projection; but (and this is a very important "but") it is projection with high degree of personal insight and sensitivity to one's self as well as to others."

(Dr. Pat Santy, 2006)

Dr. Santy's narrative is an intensive explanation of the delicate balance between the thinking and feeling aspects of working with a client. Professionals must have the insight for self-examination when they find themselves experiencing their own personal feeling states about the client's story or behavior. Countertransference can take a very destructive turn in the *helping* relationship if the *helper* is struggling with Vicarious Trauma. Here is a submission from a lawyer who has worked in the field of family law for over thirty years:

"I have been a family law lawyer for over thirty years. I represent only women in divorce cases and encounter many who have little if any experience in managing their own financial affairs. When I first started in this field, it was hard for me not to be judgmental of these women. Maybe that's because my own wife is a very capable and highly successful business person. She is

strong, decisive, and fiercely independent. It's funny that I ended up building a practice that focused on representing exactly the opposite kind of gal.

The case that stuck with me over many years is the one that involved a lady named Belle. Belle was married for thirty-eight years and had four children. She was a society lady of sorts, with a butler, two housekeepers, and a ground- skeeper. She even had a chauffeur and a chef. She wanted for nothing. Her husband had an affair with a younger woman and filed suit for a divorce. Belle completely fell apart. She appeared in my office with barely the ability to speak, shaking with anxiety and couldn't figure out how she would survive without Harvey. She lamented that Harvey took care of everything: the bills, the house, vacation planning, even picked out her wardrobe and had it sent directly to the home. He planned all the social events and made her life seem like it came out of a fairy tale. She could not understand what she did wrong.

Over the course of time I worked with her, it appeared I was her surrogate husband. She called for every decision, including what to wear for the first court appearance. She came to the office with several "appropriate" selections for my perusal.

I found myself growing more and more irritated with what I perceived to be her meaningless phone calls and idiotic questions. One particular afternoon, I finally took her call after refusing to respond to the first ten. She wanted to know what time she should have her chauffeur pick her up from our first settlement conference scheduled for the next morning. I felt a strong visceral reaction. My heart was pumping and my breathing was heavy. I was literally seeing stars. I told her I would have to call her back about the time, just so that I could take a moment and compose myself. I almost slammed the phone down at the end of that call. I frightened myself with my reaction. I had to take some time and get introspective.

What the hell was going on?! Why was this call different from all the others? I decided to call this psychologist who I regularly use as a professional witness in divorce cases and shared with him the exaggerated reaction I was having with this client. We went to college together, so he knows me pretty well. He started to laugh. I told him that I didn't think it was funny.

After he apologized, he reminded me of when, back in college, my parents were divorcing and how my mother tormented me daily with phone calls and streams of questions about the minutia of her life. But, what he remembered most was my impatience and disappointment in her lack of ability to pull herself up and take charge of her life. He explained transference and countertransference to me and he told me it was normal. He also reminded me to deal with my own "historical irritation" and leave it out of the client-lawyer relationship. I realized then, if I needed to set a boundary with Belle, I should take a half hour with her and nicely do just that."

Stanley, Family Law Attorney

Stanley was fortunate to have so readily at hand a mental health professional he was comfortable consulting, and who could reframe his agitation into something more meaningful and productive. Many *helping* professionals either do not have that luxury or are fearful and resistant to ask for help. Instead, they have a countertransference reaction and have to repress it, experience the brain strain and endure how that strain affects their physiology and their psyche.

Remember that countertransference is considered "normal" in that any *helping* relationship can take on the unconscious undertone of a surrogate family system. For example, if you are helping someone whose personality reminds you of a critical parent, your brain activity will include stimulation of the hippocampus (memory center) and those historical neurons will travel your brain just as if you were a child again, standing before that parent and having all the uncomfortable feeling states you had with that parent long ago. The necessity around this phenomenon is to face and turn into, as opposed to avoid, these normal reactions and body memories so that they may be acknowledged and respected for what they truly are and to utilize them to be of help rather than hindrance to the client.

CHAPTER SEVEN

The Miracle Worker Reverie

The Miracle Worker Reverie is an altered state of consciousness that *helpers* unwittingly enter into in order to counteract their unconscious experience of the most foundational symptoms of Vicarious Trauma – compromised safety and self-esteem needs. After years of witnessing secondary trauma with controlled empathy, *helpers* frequently find themselves compromised physically, emotionally and spiritually without recognizing they are suffering from Vicarious Trauma. The affliction of untreated Vicarious Trauma plummets them into a bitter transition in their worldview. As a result, they are at great risk for only feeling good when they perceive themselves as miracle workers, effecting amazing solutions and making huge dramatic life changes for their clients.

Helpers, in their own mind and the mind of the client, become god-like and omnipotent. This thinking is in direct opposition to a healthy worldview or spiritual outlook. Taking on this type of miracle worker persona is an unhealthy defense that our heroes believe counterbalances their deteriorative view of the world. Vicarious Trauma transforms their view of the world into a dark, unsafe and nasty place – an angry, threatening place where life as they know it can be taken away with a board complaint or a lawsuit from an unhappy client. There is no trust, there is no hope and there is no faith.

As an alternate way of dealing with their compromised esteem needs, *helpers* go into the Miracle Worker Reverie, which becomes the inverse mind state that counteracts feeling like a powerless, flawed human being. Unfortunately, they address the problem by creating another problem.

The treatment of Vicarious Trauma demands that we examine our motivation for engaging in this type of work. We need to understand that we tend to cope by turning off our own negative feeling states. One convoluted way to contain these negative feelings and perceptions is to overcompensate by becoming Miracle Workers. This is a method of distraction from Vicarious Trauma in which *helpers* feel exalted and put on a pedestal by the client or they feel exalted and put themselves on a pedestal in their own minds. At this point, one of the compelling reasons to remain in the role as a professional *helper* is for the "payback" of feeling euphoric profound ecstasy by believing we perform acts of supernatural quality for another person. Unfortunately, there is nothing spiritual about it, it is actually ego driven. This is a posturing of superiority which covers a damaged and extremely vulnerable concept of self.

Ironically, one of the symptoms of Post Traumatic Stress Disorder is feeling impervious or above human frailty. When people have near death experiences, the residual trauma includes a period of time where they see themselves as superhuman, unable to be hurt or wounded. We see an interesting dynamic that is shared by Post Traumatic Stress Disorder and Vicarious Trauma.

The problem with Miracle Worker Reverie is that it compromised the true nature of the therapeutic alliance which is built upon rapport, trust and positive regard. This alliance becomes undermined by the *helper's* need for power, control and superiority in order to maintain the Reverie. This robs clients of their therapeutic right to have their healing put in their own hands. *Helpers* often keep their clients in therapy or in protracted litigation not for the client's benefit but for the benefit, either emotional or financial, of *helpers* themselves. The belief is if *helpers* discharge the client, that client may not be able to make it on their own and that they need the *helper* to survive and make good decisions. In other words, the *helper* will save them because they cannot save themselves. It is ethically necessary for *helpers* to view the client from a strength perspective, helping the client to develop a self-perception that he or she is capable of surviving on their own.

One of the most significant dangers in what we are referring to is that, as this compulsive behavior pattern continues, *helpers* are unaware of their limitations in serving clients. When they are lost in the Miracle Worker Reverie, they do not see the benefit of referring the client out to a more competent *helper* or terminating with the client because treatment is complete. Clients then begin to serve the ego needs of *helpers* and the clients' treatment is severely compromised. The Miracle Worker Reverie can seduce a *helper* into losing professional perspective, forgetting spiritual point-of-view and increasing the risk for bad practice or practice outside the *helper's* level of expertise.

Here is a sobering account of one psychiatrist's experience with this phenomenon:

"I no longer practice medicine, and I've learned it was all of my own doing. I've come to understand where I went wrong and how I could have had the life I dreamed of and actually lived for a short time.......until I lost perspective and forfeited a fantastic opportunity. I was one of only two child and adolescent psychiatrists in my area. I was well-trained, well-respected and launching a new private practice. I took a huge risk to buy a building and launch a psychiatric practice based on the hope that things would work out in a positive manner. I hired exceptional administrative and professional staff to work with me so that the client experience from beginning to end was stellar. Soon I developed an intricate professional network, built an excellent professional reputation and gathered many referrals from numerous resources throughout my community. I was working very hard and seeing triple what was considered to be a normal caseload. I quickly was seen as the doctor for hopeless cases resulting in many resistant and difficult to treat cases sent in my direction. I welcomed them all. I was working 100 hour weeks, but at the time, perceived it to be extraordinary because I could buy vacation homes, fancy cars, artwork, boats, even a private jet for my family's personal use. My wife and children spent summers at the beach and I worked day and night to pay for their comfort. Now, in retrospect, I cannot believe the burden of caseloads I was shouldering and the internalization of horrific patient narratives I was suffering from. I was playing God and from this position of power, I was building my kingdom. I'm not exactly sure when my relationships broke down, or when my grandiosity took over, but I found myself alone, isolated and binging on seeing more and more patients to make myself feel powerful and revered. I noticed my staff beginning to complain about their workloads which I either ignored or minimized. I fired those who could not keep up with my expectations. I became so over-focused on building a huge practice that I became much less attentive to important ethical aspects of maintaining such a practice. A primary example of this was my attitude toward insurance claims and the filing thereof. I complained bitterly that my staff wasn't getting their patients in often enough for therapy and that the billings were down. Eventually fraudulent insurance claims were filed. I created my own prison in that with all my power came a pervasive isolation. I was a prisoner of my own success. I felt I couldn't ask others for support, supervision or input on a case. I was the great and brilliant psychiatrist. How could I ask for help? I am not proud of what happened to me. I lost my practice, my family, my reputation and my medical license. I spent years in treatment with a psychiatrist who understood the concept of Vicarious Trauma. It is no excuse, but had I understood the damaging impact of working too hard and internalizing years worth of traumatic stories, I might have stayed more conscious of my

own limitations. At the time, I distracted myself from this realization by seeing myself as omnipotent and building myself an empire. I believed I could save all those patients. I was the only one who could do it and I let them all down. But worse, I let myself and my family down. It's been a long road back."

Thomas, Psychiatrist

The ego-driven compulsion behind Miracle Worker Reverie needs to be understood and addressed. Thomas was driven by the power of the financial, emotional, professional and egotistical rewards of his successes in being seen as a miracle worker. His loss of perspective was his downfall. The inability to debrief his traumas led him to distract himself and become overzealous in his quest for greatness. His ability to prioritize became negatively affected and his professional judgment suffered. He lost sight of his original motivation, which was to become a psychiatrist to serve people suffering with emotional disorders. As a result, he lost everything, including his giving human spirit. His addiction to helping, which was about him, prevented him from being a true agent of growth and change for his patients. His compulsion for helping was ultimately not for the benefit of the clients; instead, it became his own personal addiction with the payback never being quite enough, much like a drug. Drugs wear off after awhile and the user needs more (recognition), and more (money), and more (power). Worse, the tolerance for the pain from the stories we hear becomes higher and higher and the Vicarious Trauma intensifies unknowingly until it has destroyed its victim.

CHAPTER EIGHT

Rapid Advance Process for Vicarious Trauma Relief

Now that we have become aware of the many factors that set the stage for our heroes to fall prey to the misery of Vicarious Trauma, it is time to discuss an effective, brief approach to its treatment. We have talked about how neuroscience demonstrates that chronic stress injures and changes the structure of the brain. The strain of Vicarious Trauma also inhibits neurogenesis or the birth of new neurons. Vicarious Trauma victims need to recognize that new brain cells can come into a complicated, ingrained, and negative brain circuitry and become part of that circuitry in a restorative way (Begley, 2007).

Since we have come to understand that the brain damage of Vicarious Trauma is experienced as a painful inner transformation in the individual's identity, perhaps the greatest negative impact can be described as a break to the essence or the spirit of the individual. After internalizing *trauma content* stories over time through the strain of controlled empathy, it should not be surprising that *helping* professionals find themselves poor or broken in spirit. Their core spiritual identity, their basic essence, becomes inaccessible to them.

The spirit of a *helping* individual can be identified as the level of consciousness that rises above upset and stress and responds to negative situations with dynamics such as courage, faith, hope, trust and forgiveness. The neurocircuitry of trauma makes accessing the higher brain without a conscious and concerted effort very challenging. When people are in disconnect from this powerful higher perspective, they are left with limbic brain reactions such as fear and anxiety as their primary context for perceiving the world. They become stuck in self-definition that is negative and judgmental.

Vicarious Trauma leaves the individual at great risk to be in separation from the spiritual perspective or the higher brain. An individual's sense of spiritual identity is sacred unto itself and is free from self-judgment. Vicarious Trauma puts the *helper* in the position of self-regard that attacks the fundamental nature of *helpers* and states: "I am powerless, I am depressed, I am all-powerful, I am a god." Treatment must include a viable method for bridging back to the higher mind so *helpers* can remain healthy, centered, open, neutral, and positive in their work. Vicarious Trauma precipitates an impasse in the *helper's* Spiritual Bridge or neural pathways to that higher level of consciousness. Recovery from Vicarious Trauma must include some way to mend that impasse and restore the neural pathways to the higher left-brain or the spiritual perspective.

We believe that recovery from Vicarious Trauma is possible for any *helping* professional. In our extensive research of Vicarious Trauma combined with our own experience with it, we came to understand that a need existed for effective treatment. Subsequently, we developed a brief and effective process that the *helper* can utilize entirely on their own – the **Rapid Advance Process**.

The **Rapid Advance Process** consists of five steps for Vicarious Trauma recovery:

Step 1:   Reveal the History

Step 2:   Recognize the Impasse

Step 3:   Release the Past

Step 4:   Respond to Fear

Step 5:   Reconnect with the Higher Mind

Before we launch into the steps, we want the reader to know how this book is structured to best benefit you. The remainder of this chapter explains the five steps of the **Rapid Advance Process**; then, the second half of the book contains the **AFTER-SHOCK Workbook**, which was written for you to work through after reading this chapter.

STEP 1

Reveal the History

IT WAS

As evidence has shown, a little more than half of *helping* professionals have reported themselves as trauma survivors. We can estimate that the actual number is higher than that since many *helpers* do not disclose their own trauma histories. Most *helping* professionals are highly skilled at controlled empathy because they have survived their own trauma histories and have become proficient at exercising emotional control. They have also developed a high tolerance for *trauma content*. Nonetheless, consciousness of what is going on for them unconsciously is critical in warding off the insidiousness of Vicarious Trauma. The countertransference phenomenon can only be brought to consciousness by revealing the *helper's* own history which is being stimulated by the hippocampus and amygdala of the *helper's* brain, as the story of the client is unfolding.

The *helping* professional, like everyone else, has a very important and revealing personal history called childhood. Time must be taken to seriously consider it and to study it. Many *helpers* have forgotten much of their own painful past or perhaps have developed a selective recall about it. Now we're not suggesting that the professional become bogged down in the past – far from it. Instead, we are suggesting that they review the past and use it as a catalyst to counteract the effects of countertransference which leads to Vicarious Trauma.

We are not suggesting that the past was all bad. The good stuff simply is not our concern right now. What we are interested in is how your memory of some upsetting events may be at risk of being triggered through your work, thereby incurring some breaks or impasses in your own Spiritual Bridge or neural pathways to your higher mind. This impasse negatively affects your belief system, core identity and inner sense of well-being. It also interferes with your ability to function at optimum level in your profession.

As *helping* professionals, many of us already believe that children are considered "impressionable" because, when they first enter the world, they can be considered almost an entirely spiritual self because they are very much centered in the present. Babies have virtually no sense of the intellectual, physical or emotional selves. As infants begin to move through the oversized, scary world, those dimensions of self begin to develop. This, for the most part, is as it is supposed to be, except when the Spiritual Self which only knows acceptance, innocence, goodness and love, is sacrificed to the development of the physical, emotional and intellectual selves. This development at the sacrifice of the Spiritual Self is also called the ego. When children develop an ego, they are converting to a fear-based way of thinking that is virtually opposed to the powerful spiritual component. This unconscious process happens to all of us. That's just the way it is. As we develop into adulthood the brain submerges painful memories through the hippocampus and we become like an onion with layers of defense over these disturbing memories.

Some people appear to be more separated from their Spiritual Selves than others. The depth of the **impasse** or break in the Spiritual Bridge (the neural pathways to the higher brain) depends on the intensity of the historical fear to which the child was initially subjected. What you will come to understand is that no matter how wide the gap, reconnecting is equally easy for everyone. You simply need to acknowledge that the break did occur, that it recurs through your work, and then make the personal commitment to reconnect.

Unfortunately, too many of us remain unaware of unconscious reactions to clients' *trauma content*. That's why you are reading this book – to become consciously aware of what is unconsciously going on as a form of personal and professional empowerment. When *helpers* are in a place where an historical fear is unconsciously triggered, it can be torturous. The inclination of *helpers* is not unlike the predicament of Superman. Superman was a miracle worker; all powerful, as long as he was out of the range of kryptonite. If kryptonite was close by, he could still function as long as it was enclosed in lead. Our personal historical fears are our emotional kryptonite. Our denial, in whatever form it takes, is the lead box. We operate powerfully as *helpers* until some traumatic client story we absorb flips the lid open on the lead box. Then watch out! We are at risk to feel threatened and personally paralyzed and powerless.

Now, some of you may be saying, "This is hopeless. How could I ever overcome the constant risk of being traumatized through my work?" Don't worry. That feeling of hopelessness is a great indicator of your own personal separation from your higher brain. Remember that hope is a higher-mind, spiritually-based behavior. It is easy to get back to hopefulness.

The intensity of the negative historical experience triggered is actually irrelevant. An historical experience is a memory and nothing more. It lurks around in the recesses of our minds. It simply does not exist in the present. The particular meaning of any memory is the meaning we choose to ascribe to it. We can change the meaning at any time. You'll have to decide when you are ready to change the meaning of a memory. But first, you'll have to acknowledge it.

Reframing a painful past experience in terms of a spiritual break motivates us to change its impact. Once you can accept that the force of Vicarious Trauma precipitates a separation from the higher mind, reconnecting is similarly restorative for everyone. Operating from the spiritual perspective of self-acceptance, rather than the ego-based perspective of fear, restores us as *helpers* to our original transparent identity and places a painful event, be it the clients' or our own, in the position of nothing more than a statement of what was.

Your personal history is important to keep in mind as you work because it is where you began to make judgment about yourself and your place in the world as you moved through those early experiences. It was the decision making place for what became the objects of your faith – for what you believe and for what you have unconsciously set up and lived out through the course of your life. Conscious or not, your childhood experiences get triggered through the course of your work. Your own child-like reactions to *trauma content* are also triggered. This creates a brain strain in the mid portions of your brain, where raw feelings emerge. If you are working a lot, you probably have a neural pattern that prohibits you from accessing your higher thinking, where you could provide yourself some healing, comforting thoughts and emotions.

STEP 2

Recognizing the Impasse
IT IS

History repeats itself. We can remember many times when we as children swore to ourselves that we would never say to our own children some of the inane things our mothers and fathers said to us. We humble ourselves before you now as we confess to the number of times we have nearly had to gag ourselves in order not to say to our kids exactly what our mothers and fathers said to us! Similarly, those who have unresolved fears about the past are at risk to repeat it. We repeat it in our primary "relationships", in our parenting, in the workplace and in our friendships. The tendency to do this is unconscious, yet seductive and addictive. We will actually attract personality types into our experiences that are easy targets for the projections of our childhood fears.

So let's take a trip down memory lane and look closely at where you have been. You've been in your mother's womb, in her arms and in the arms of others. You were really small when the rest of the world seemed really big and your little eyes perceived many things as larger than life itself. You have probably forgotten about all that over the years. To quickly remember, simply take a second, put the book down and squat down close to the floor and look all around you. Quite a different perspective, wouldn't you say? Have you ever visited a kindergarten or first grade classroom? The chairs and desks are so tiny, so close to the floor. The drinking fountain lies low as well. You perceived early that certain things, certain people, certain places were big and scary and you didn't like that feeling of fear, so you buried it. A child automatically does this as a survival mechanism. After all, how can a defenseless child survive in a scary world? He can't. So in order to keep away from the feeling of fear, you began to develop certain **acting-in** or **acting-out** behaviors as a way to distract yourself from unpleasant feelings. You might have sucked your thumb, had nightmares, or wet the bed. Perhaps you had temper tantrums, were painfully shy, or you were aggressive with other children. Maybe you did poorly in school or not as well as you might have. Maybe you got sick a lot. Conceivably, you were too competitive or not competitive enough. These behaviors served as distractions from the unpleasant feeling of fear. Take a minute to recall some of your childhood traits and behaviors. They were the seedlings of traits and behaviors you possess today. Some of them are great. Some of them are huge obstacles in the way of remembering who you really are. An understanding of how they evolved empowers you to decide, in the present, which were useful and which were not.

The self-protective distractions of our childhood "mature" as we develop. A thumb sucker may develop into an alcohol/drug abuser. A painfully shy child may develop into a depressed adult. A wounded child might develop into a savior. Although these are a little more sophisticated, they are distractions all the same and we re-create the past with the help of our distractions. Once our history has been revealed, we are able to get conscious about or recognize how we repeatedly find ourselves at the impasse in adulthood and more so, through our work.

Fear-based relationships can be further explored by looking at Dr. Eric Berne's (1964) Drama Triangle. The Drama Triangle is drawn from Berne's concept of Transactional Analysis. Visualize, if you will, a triangle with three different roles, one at each point. The first is the victim position. The second is the rescuer position, and the third is the perpetrator position. When we are stuck in a fear-based perspective, we are at risk of moving around this dysfunctional system with our clients, continually interchanging the roles.

DRAMA TRIANGLE

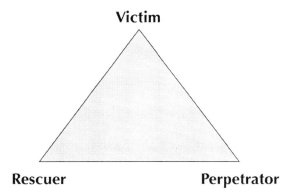

A medical doctor, James came to see us because he said he was having marital problems. There were problems all along in the four years he was with Krista, but things had really escalated when she got the phone bill and found out that he had made a series of calls to a 1-800 phone porn service. Krista shoved the bill at James and told him to get some help or she was filing for divorce. James wasn't very enthused about working with us at first because he was very ashamed of his "presenting problem". He also saw himself as a "Miracle Worker" who ran a huge clinic for the poor. He was above needing help and felt like he was being bullied by his wife into seeking treatment. We pointed out to him that he was a very bright man and he certainly knew that he would be caught when the phone bill arrived. We interpreted the acting-out behavior not so much as a sexual addiction but as a clear cry for some help. James listened to hundreds of traumatic stories at work and never considered the possibility of Vicarious Trauma. James felt relieved when it was put that way and he began to talk.

James spent most of his time at the clinic and saw many people who were chronically ill due to traumatic circumstances: no homes, no money, hard drugs, rape, and assault. One patient, in particular, preyed on his mind constantly. She would come to the clinic no less than four times a week with many maladies that were the result of very poor living conditions and very poor nutrition. James would spend a great deal of time being a compassionate ear for this woman. She had given birth to a son seven years ago as a result of being raped by someone she knew in her tenement. Due to the circumstances of his creation, she didn't care for this child. The habit she formed to avoid taking care of him was by being chronically ill herself and incapacitated in her role as mother.

James was a quiet, gentle kind of guy who tended to keep to himself. Of course, the more he kept to himself, the more the story of the chronically ill lady rolled around in his mind. He became shut down in his marriage. The more shut-down he became, the more his wife came after him complaining that she did not receive enough love, affection, or intimacy.

James shared with us that he would really dissociate when Krista got sick. When she had a cold or the flu, rather than be helpful, he would be indifferent, which really sent his wife into orbit. Rather than help his poor wife out, James felt put upon by Krista to take responsibility for her health. He resented her illness and distracted himself by becoming depressed. Finally, he chose a more covert way to express his anger to his wife. His attempt to get her attention worked. James was putting his marriage and his career at risk with his porn phone calls. He was a victim of Vicarious Trauma and he didn't even know it.

Revealing the history really helped us to get a handle on the situation. James was the last born, only male in a family of three children. His mother was an "invalid" who was chronically sick, in bed most of the time and very powerful in her supine position. To this day, no one is certain about exactly what is wrong with her. The father dedicated his entire life to nursing the woman and her poor health set the tone for how the family system would evolve. The children were expected to keep quiet and take care of themselves lest mother have a setback and the father had no needs in the marriage because it would be absurd to expect anything from a partner who was unable to function. James recalled feeling cheated and ignored as a child. He had no relationship with his mother and was more of a parent to his father in being cooperative with father's need to play nurse. This was the memory embedded in his hippocampus.

James recognized the impasse to his higher brain that got triggered by his relationship with the chronically ill woman at the clinic. Choosing a career in medicine seemed logical after he revealed his own history. He also recognized how the drama triangle had unconsciously been created in his life. Working at the clinic made him vulnerable to Vicarious Trauma.

His **acting-in** distraction of depression and his **acting-out** distraction of phone sex helped keep him dissociated from some very painful historical feelings that were being triggered by his work. He postponed having this upset for many years. Not surprisingly, James did not give much consideration to his spiritual identity and he reported doing nothing in the way of nurturing his Spiritual Self. That didn't surprise us. You can't nurture something to which you are not connected. Maternal abandonment, no matter what form it takes, is a severe break to the Spiritual Bridge or the neural pathway to the higher brain. James went from an innocent sense of identity to one of feeling abandoned and unworthy. James could not trust women, he had no faith in healthy love, he did not have courage to state his position and ask to have his needs met, and last but not least, he was prohibiting himself from accessing forgiveness because he had not yet acknowledged his anger, sadness, and shame. James looked calm and happy, but behind the gentle exterior was a very angry and sad man.

Once we recognize the impasse, triggered by Vicarious Trauma, we also notice that we basically move around in a constant state of separation anxiety. Traditionally, separation anxiety is a term that refers to the upset a child feels when he/she must detach from a parent. We believe that *all* anxiety is actually separation anxiety, since we define separation anxiety as the chronic underlying distress we feel as a result of being separated from the most loving and nurturing **spiritual** part of *ourselves*. This sensitivity is as unpleasant in adulthood as it was in childhood and we stick to certain distractions as a way to avoid feeling it. Separation anxiety would keep us trapped inside the Drama Triangle, a fear-based system. Recognizing and meeting this anxiety enables us to get out of the triangle altogether.

Those of us attached to the past are bound to unconsciously re-create it. We've been doing it for so long we don't even notice it anymore. It also carries an addictive quality to it. The familiarity of being stuck there has a perverse sense of comfort simply because we are so connected to the associated unpleasant feeling states. *Recognizing* when we are replaying an updated version of an historical scene, and *experiencing*, rather than avoiding the separation anxiety that gets triggered in the replay, are some very important skills in mending the Spiritual Bridge. **Recognizing the Impasse** is the wake-up call to do something different. *Experiencing* our separation anxiety motivates us to consciously work on reconnecting to the higher brain. When we reconnect to the Spiritual Self, we realize that we are never abandoned and, therefore, never alone. Resolving feelings of isolation is a powerful counterpoint to the symptoms of Vicarious Trauma.

STEP 3

Releasing the Past

I CAN

Our unconscious attachment to some aspect of a painful past prohibits our bridging to the higher brain or spiritual self. This self is an inner consciousness that stays peacefully centered in the here and now. Having, to this point, determined an impasse and decided to no longer retreat from it, we can now begin to mend the break in our Spiritual Bridge. This is experienced as a challenge because we are in the midst of Vicarious Trauma and separation anxiety at the time we call upon ourselves to begin the repair. Traditional psychology would coin this "free-floating anxiety". It is free-floating in that as we let go of our denial and defensiveness, we fear drifting off into oblivion due to disconnection. We can now take a leap of faith that in letting go we give ourselves back to our higher mind and protect ourselves from the danger of Vicarious Trauma.

When we release the past, we release ourselves to exchange our purpose. As we give fear over to a higher form of thinking, we receive spiritually based dynamics in ourselves. When we exchange our purpose, we change our mind from *separation through fear* to *connection through hope and peacefulness*. This exchange fosters resilience. We transform the objects of our faith by no longer inspiring the painful past through the trauma stories of others. Unpleasant feeling states are no longer the foundation of our beliefs. Instead, the higher mind, the spiritual self, is where we extend ourselves to keep personal vigil. We begin to form more healing neural pathways and can negotiate trauma material more resourcefully.

What exactly is the past? It is typically defined as the time before or time gone by. What does that mean? The past is a span of time. Is it tangible? We don't think so. Our memories of times gone by are all that really exist and they exist only in our minds. Memories are not really the past – they are only perceptions of it. It is important to realize that what we remember has far less impact than how we remember it. The historical action is over. It is only our judgment of it that actually remains. In a family, a parent's memory may be very different from a child's. For example, a mother might perceive the family as having been wonderful with her role as parent as having been very positive and helpful. While a child of that mother may perceive the opposite. The child may have perceived it as unsafe, with that same mother as a scary woman! Who was right and who was wrong? Neither, yet both. In many situations a child's release from historical pain is found in the understanding that his or her memory of Mom's behavior was his or hers own alone. An adult child can exchange his or her purpose from *fear* to *forgiveness* and in so doing, relinquish the self-judgment that in light of a painful memory, he or she was unworthy of receiving love.

The point is that a perception of the past exists in our minds and that is all there is left of it. The events themselves are much less meaningful than how you absorbed the events as they occurred. How you took them in, experienced them, processed them and judged yourself in their context is what makes up your perception of them. You can change your perception any time you choose to relinquish judgment. When you reframe your perception of the past, you transform your neural circuitry around the memory, thereby releasing it.

Now, we realize there are many people at the impasse and we can hear the balking: "Right, Vicki and Ellie! My father called me a whore and a slut. You're saying that *I* have a faulty perception of that verbal abuse?!" Yes, your Father *did* verbally abuse you and it appears he's still doing it, only now he has your permission to do so. You see, the verbal attack no longer exists. Only your perception of it remains. It is important to grasp that the attack itself never had any meaning. The way you *felt* at the time it happened imparts the only meaning the attack has. How did you feel when you were being attacked? Scared, sad, angry and shameful probably describe your feelings. What have you done about those feelings? Distracted yourself through some *acting-in* or *acting-out* behavior that includes healing the pain of others.

Furthermore, you are at risk of taking that painful perception of the past and projecting it onto people and circumstances today in a counterproductive fashion. This can happen to you within the *helping* relationship through the phenomenon of counter-transference. Those negative historical feelings are still there and because you don't attend to them, you are stuck with a perception of the past that undoubtedly gets played out again and again in the here and now. So your father still verbally abuses you, only now he has your permission to do so. Such complicity is not the healthy, healing way to deal with a painful history.

Forgiveness, the relinquishment of historical judgment followed by a thought of peace, is the binding material of the Spiritual Bridge. It is the stuff that keeps the bridge intact as a span to the higher brain or spiritual self. Without forgiveness, there will always be an impasse in the Bridge, making it impossible to reconnect to our greatest internal resource in the struggle against Vicarious Trauma. **Releasing the Past** requires the first step of forgiveness. **Responding to Fear** requires the second.

Forgiveness includes the correction of one's perception through the relinquishment of judgment. The events of our past and the past of our clients are not the obstacle in letting go, rather it is our repeated decision to cast judgment on ourselves and the people connected to the events that detain us in it, sometimes for a lifetime. The choice to judge someone as good or bad, right or wrong, starts with judging ourselves.

Kayleigh, a social worker, came to our center because she was having difficulty shaking off a deep depression she reported having since she heard the devastating client story about the serious illness of the client's first child. Shortly after the birth of her child, the client noticed that the baby was not thriving. A heart defect had gone undetected at birth. The client was on government assistance because of poverty and was really struggling to get some medical care for her baby. By the time she got in to see Kayleigh, the baby was seriously ill. Kayleigh wanted to help and became highly anxious as she battled the bureaucratic government red tape on behalf of her client. She noticed her depression deepening every time she met with this client.

We were able to quickly identify the countertransference. Kayleigh herself had a son named Todd who died from heart failure at the age of seventeen. He originally had two holes in his heart at birth and was operated on at age two to repair the holes. When the doctors started his heart back up, it would not beat on its own, so they implanted a pacemaker that seemed to do the trick. Todd lived a "normal" life until he suddenly and unexpectedly died during class at school.

Kayleigh shared in her third session that she was the first-born to a very shaming, controlling mother. When she entered into adolescence, mom began to attack her regarding her behavior with boys. Rather than sit and have an informative talk about the birds and the bees, she threatened Kayleigh about promiscuity and suggested to her daughter that she was provocative and "loose" with pubescent young men. Kayleigh finally embodied Mother's theme by becoming pregnant at sixteen. The young man involved with the pregnancy brought her a "morning after pill" when she told him the news. He advised her that when she took the pill, she would begin to bleed and lose the pregnancy. She was so terrified to be pregnant and judged as shameful, she swallowed it. Nothing happened. Kayleigh met someone on the beach a few weeks later. He married her and claimed the pregnancy as a result of their marriage. Todd was born with a major birth defect for which Kayleigh blamed herself. When Todd died, she began distracting herself from this devastation by helping others.

The first time we met with her, she commented about the unattractive place-ment of the furniture. Shortly thereafter, she remarked angrily that Ellie was looking out the window. The second session, she began to pre-empt feedback by saying things like, "Now don't go saying any of that stupid 'You are a good person and you're okay' psycho-garbage to me!" Vicki took in a relaxing breath as I looked at her and responded, "Kayleigh, I wasn't going to say anything of the sort. I am having a reaction and I need to take a risk with you. My percep-tion of some of your behaviors in building a relationship with us is that you are trying to connect to us in shame. Some judgmental remarks have tipped us off to this style. If you are being judgmental with us, then we imagine that you must be very judgmental with yourself. Perhaps this is a style you re-create from mother's role modeling." Kayleigh settled into her chair. "Yes", she said, "I am just like her and I hate myself for it." She had a confused expression on her face as we remarked, "So, are you now judging yourself for being judgmental?" She laughed for the first time since we had met and its tone was melodious. "I sure am, aren't I?"

Then we all laughed together as some healing was taking place. When we are fearful and separated, we tend to beat on ourselves unmercifully. We need to remember that our purpose here on earth is certainly not to abuse ourselves.

When we are in a state of fear and shame we cannot access the neutrality of spiritual thinking. When we are connected to the higher mind, we realize we should not judge the client's behaviors or our own. In giving up judgment, we merely give up what we never had a right to in the first place. Furthermore, when we operate from the higher mind, we can observe things from a higher consciousness that knows no separation. Through spiritual exercise, neural activity intensifies in the prefrontal cortex and the *helper* can utilize these restored pathways to find the intrinsic meaning behind their own suffering and the suffering of others. This healing replaces the ineffective process of judgmental thinking.

Forgiveness is for people, not for actions. When we are faced with an awful mistake, be it our own or someone else's, it would be far more effective to forgive ourselves and/or the other person and give the mistake over to the universe. The relinquish-ment of judgment invites wisdom in to handle the problem. When you forgive in this manner, watch the course of events that follow as they work in a way to rectify the mistake. Holding onto judgment simply keeps breathing life into the trauma so that we perceive it happening over and over and over.

Kayleigh was given a homework assignment. She was asked to consider the events of her own past without any self-judgment. As she practiced this, she realized that she was at an impasse in her Spiritual Bridge because of Vicarious Trauma. She faced her separation anxiety rather than retreat from it through depression. She took a leap of faith and exchanged her purpose from self-abuse to connecting with her higher mind. She relinquished judgment, and therefore, changed her mind. As Kayleigh became more centered on mending her Spiritual Bridge, her Vicarious Trauma symptoms diminished. She became less depressed, less isolated and, not coincidentally, she met a woman at work who shared that she, too, had lost a child. Kayleigh helped her colleague bring the loss to closure through forgiveness and peace. She also began strengthening her relationships with her two younger daughters, who really needed the unconditional love of an available mother. She let herself heal and its effects extended out to heal the lives of her clients. Spiritual Bridging makes healthy alliances.

When was the last time you forgave yourself for struggling in your work? When was the last time you asked forgiveness for a mistake you made, remembering that you are worthy of forgiveness? Maybe you haven't thought about this. We all suffer because unforgiving behaviors have created a professional mentality that dictates *attack, be attacked, or avoid it all and take no risks.* Fear-based thinking sets professionals up to feel ashamed of themselves when they are experiencing Vicarious Trauma, rather than to be accepting, self-compassionate and open to seeking help.

Did you know you could be forgiven without formally saying you are sorry? Did you know that you can forgive someone who has never apologized to you? Nothing does your heart more good than to forgive yourself for some mistake, such as where you say to another, "I've acted like such a jerk. Will you forgive me?" However, certain mistakes we can no longer rectify in person. For these, we must choose to forgive ourselves.

Forgiveness is purely a reciprocal process. When you forgive yourself, the other involved is forgiven as well. Every time you forgive yourself, you see the meaning in forgiving others. When you forgive others, you are no longer attached to them through fear and shame. Collaborations in fear and shame precipitate more of the same and draw in a lot of negativity. These types of attachments imprison us in trauma symptoms and prohibit us from realizing the power of the spiritual perspective.

Justification is the obstacle to forgiveness. We think we have the right to bear a grievance based on our perceptions of trauma. Our perceptions are points of view, not absolute truth. Justification is the misuse of the intellectual self to set up a distraction from our own fearful separation anxiety. We are so used to pain and suffering that, unconsciously, we practically worship them. If we were to give them up, we believe there would be a huge inner void. For some, the release of pain and suffering would throw them into such an identity crisis that they think there would be nothing left at all. In order to sustain a false sense of security, they unconsciously uphold fear as the object of their faith by justifying their reasons to be angry at a cruel world and to withhold forgiveness. The next time you feel very upset with someone else's traumatic story, take notice of your judgmental thinking.

Sandy, a 25-year-old lawyer, came to see us very shortly after she began working as a public defender and after her parents were divorced. Sandy became very depressed and highly volatile shortly after she was assigned a gruesome rape case where the victim was a woman close to her own age.

Sandy was actually referred to us by her mother who had been in counseling right at the time her husband left her after twenty-seven years of marriage. Her mother had a history of depression, offset by episodes of rage that were terrifying to whoever happened to be present at the time. The husband, Sandy's father, who was having a lengthy affair with a colleague, left because he was tired of caretaking what he perceived to be a non-functioning spouse. In their years together, he was constantly walking on eggshells around his wife, being the proverbial nice guy and not rocking the boat. During all their years together, he never asked her to stop.

Sandy's mother was a second-born daughter and Sandy was also a second-born daughter. Her mother fared very well in treatment and when she eventually left treatment, she had a home of her own, a full-time job as supervisor for a four-star resort and a sense of peacefulness and power over her life.

Sandy's presenting problem of work-related stress unveiled her recent memory of an unfortunate turn of events when at the age of sixteen she and her partner went to a party with Sandy's older sister. There, she became very drunk and revealed to her sister that she was gay. Sandy then had a forceful argument with her partner, left the party, and hailed a cab to get her home. She started conversing with the driver and reported to him that she was gay.

After the cab passed the road to her house, Sandy realized she was not going home. The driver took her to a desolate spot and raped her. Being drunk, Sandy was unable to fight him off. Sandy was in deep emotional crisis about recovering this memory at the time she came in. The part of this presenting problem that piqued my curiosity was that after the episode, she went directly home and showered for two hours. Why would a highly intelligent woman, who is an activist for feminine rights, destroy important physical evidence that would directly lead to the arrest of her assailant?

The rape case Sandy was assigned was traumatizing and triggering old business for Sandy. The explanation was found once we revealed the history. In the course of growing up, she felt extremely frightened of her mother's behavior at a very young age. She also perceived that her father was doing virtually nothing to protect her. To distract herself from her fear, Sandy took on the protective role in the family. She spent exorbitant amounts of time being the perfect child and maintaining her mother's sanity. She would interact with her mother for hours on end in an attempt to keep her steady. This was an exercise in futility since we can never really be in control of someone else's sanity. Sandy was repeatedly only as good as her last performance. The pressure was constantly on her to keep plugging away and so she did. Unfortunately, this was useless to her mother, who was enabled to never take responsibility for her own feelings and behaviors. Once the divorce took place and her mother took a turn for the better, Sandy believed she had no purpose and no identity. Behind all that, she carried a deep anger for her father and men in general, who she perceived as being very betraying and abandoning. Sandy compensated by professionally defending powerless people.

She primarily struggled with repeating "I am valueless", a judgment she made as a child who thought that if she were of any value her father certainly would have watched over and protected her. The memory of the rape with the absence of assailant accountability sustained her unconscious re-creation of male betrayal.

The fear and shame she carried from childhood flourished in the incorrect childhood perception that she in some way deserved her paternal abandonment. She judged that she was not lovable or valuable enough to receive any better. She wasn't acceptable to her personal God and this judgment she had perpetuated on her own. After the betrayal of rape, she betrayed herself by washing away important evidence. Once again, she saw herself as a victim who is powerless and out-of-control.

Sandy came to quickly understand her vulnerability for Vicarious Trauma in her work. In our time together she put her attention on letting go of her past through reciprocal forgiveness. She bridged into her own perceived void and realized it was no void at all. She understood it was a place inside that was originally meant for her spiritual self, something she had abandoned through her distraction of being the perfect child.

The rape is in the past. It is now a memory like all memories, which can be rendered meaningless through forgiveness. Sandy exchanged her purpose in counseling. She relinquished self-judgment and in so doing, corrected her trauma-based perception of the experience as a glimpse of a fear-based world where the choices were to attack, be attacked, or take no risks and avoid it all. Her new purpose inspired her to extend to her higher mind and to others by serving as a gifted criminal lawyer. Her relationship with her parents grows closer and is steadily improving.

Releasing the past through the relinquishment of judgment begins mending the impasse in the Spiritual Bridge and launches recovery from Vicarious Trauma. Now that we have exchanged our purpose and therefore changed our minds, we are ready to use thoughts of peace to change our behaviors when we are being challenged by fear and dread through the stories we hear at work.

STEP 4

Responding to Fear

I KNOW

There is a big difference between *responding* and *reacting* when we are attending to the trauma narratives of our clients. *Reacting* involves little or no spiritual connection. It is ruled by the right brain or the unconscious mind and is predicated upon neural circuitry that has been rooted in some aspect of the past. To react is to act back or to act again and can become the re-creation drama of the impasse. Reaction is defensive in nature and is based on the limbic brain's instinct of fight, flight or freeze. We react when we have a need to protect ourselves. Sometimes this is desirable. If a car is coming right at you, luckily you will react by swerving your own vehicle out of the way. In the immediacy of physically threatening situations, the fight or flight instinct kicks in automatically and is not based in hearing *trauma content* or on the projection of our pasts. Reaction skills are very useful when we find ourselves in physically dangerous circumstances.

Responding involves the introduction of a reply or an answer and is associated with the conscious, left brain. How do we answer in emotionally fearful conditions? Many of us tend to use the same fight, flight or freeze reaction in emotionally fearful circumstances. We verbally attack the fearful subject or withdraw from it. In emotionally scary circumstances with clients, neither of these reactive options is very useful simply because they breathe life into the fear and suffering they are attempting to eradicate. Attacking someone puts us in the perpetrator position. Withdrawing from someone puts us in the victim position. Either way, we keep ourselves stuck in the drama triangle and we feel a lot of pain.

> *Joan, a young nurse, thirty years old came to see us because she was still on the fence about getting a legal divorce after a seven month separation from her husband. Joan explained that she was feeling afraid to make a decision. Being officially on her own seemed frightening and giving her rageful husband the bad news seemed equally as frightening. Joan withdrew from a scary set of circumstances and the more she withdrew, the more life she breathed into her own fear.*
>
> *She was already living physically apart from her husband for seven months and she worked double shifts in the ICU to pay her living expenses. While she*

was able to live independently from a financial point of view, her controlling husband continued to keep track of the money and keep track of Joan. Joan never really moved through any of the emotional challenges of independent adult living because she still felt compelled to answer to her estranged husband about her life. Joan also chose not to face the unacceptability of her husband's abusive behavior. His aggressive behavior had a paralyzing effect on her and her decision to check out from it actually reinforced his tendency to go after her, once again breathing life into the very thing that scared her.

Joan shared with us that in her work she was particularly stressed about a 62-year-old female patient who was admitted after suffering a stroke. As the woman began the slow road to recovery, the woman's grown children told Joan numerous shocking stories about the woman's abusive marriage. Joan reported that she felt more depressed, inert, and unmotivated since she began caring for this patient.

Shortly after getting Joan's history, we were able to suggest to her that she was suffering from Vicarious Trauma. Our first point to her was that making no decision about being married was, in fact, a decision. Either you are in a relationship or you are not. She thought she was avoiding a divorce. We believed she was avoiding the marriage and that was clearly a decision not to be married. Her difficulty was not in her apparent ambivalence – her difficulty was her reacting rather than responding to her fear. Her reacting took the form of emotional paralysis. She was going through the motions of daily living like a robot, functioning well at completing necessary tasks, but dissociated and experiencing no joy in life. What was her fear? Her fear was of abandonment, the fear was being triggered through her work, and that fear had its roots in a much earlier time.

When Joan was ten years old her alcoholic, rageaholic father began to sexually molest her. This continued for about six years as Joan was threatened in a number of ways by her father if she were to ever make a fuss or tell anyone. Joan was at her father's mercy for a very long time. Adding insult to injury, Joan's mother refused to believe and protect her daughter when at the age of sixteen Joan mustered up the courage to tell her the sordid tale. Joan was trained at a young age to take flight from fear. She learned to withdraw and dissociate from a fearful situation. She buried the tragic memory of her youth. She also unconsciously re-created the history in her marriage to an abusive man, held herself at his mercy, and ironically, abandoned herself over and over again by not responding to her fears. The Vicarious Trauma she suffered through her work became her emotional tipping point and was making it impossible to keep it all together.

After we ascertained that she no longer wanted to be married, her husband escalated with inappropriate behavior. Joan commented that she was always afraid that he would react ragefully. We then pointed out that her husband's abusiveness was his problem and not hers. She took on the responsibility for his problem because that was the position she took on with her father at an earlier time in her life. Joan recognized that her fear was the fear of a defenseless little girl. She had judged herself as shameful and inadequate up to this point. She went undercover by becoming a miracle worker for those people on the brink of death.

When she relinquished self-judgment she began parenting herself very differently. She stopped working double shifts. She calmly started setting very clear boundaries with her soon-to-be ex. She filed for divorce, opened her own bank and charge accounts, and served her spouse with an order of protection. With each responsive step she took toward emotional freedom, her fear shrank respectively. She reported a sense of peacefulness about herself and her ex as she let go. She began to build confidence and started to have faith in her abilities. The burden of Vicarious Trauma transformed into a blessing, as it offered Joan a powerful opportunity to heal.

Responding to fear sustains our release of the past. Once we have relinquished the self-judgment unconsciously made in a much earlier time, we need to stay peaceful when we meet up with a scary present work situation that triggers our limbic brain. When we commit to letting go of the past by becoming conscious of it, we state "I can", which affirms our decision to no longer perceive ourselves as victims.

When fear is triggered through the *trauma content* we hear at work, we can now state that we know what is really going on. We are right at the impasse and now know what to do so that we do not turn back. We meet and rise above separation anxiety, as we remember that we are not abandoned, not alone, and we worthy of our higher mind's protective love. *Responding* rather than *reacting* implies thinking peacefully or calmly when we are deciding what to do or what to say in a scary situation.

Emotional *reacting* occurs as a result of poor impulse control. It has been found that the brain's frontal lobes, usually regarded as the set of higher order functions, forge powerful connections to the limbic system in the primitive brain. When fear is triggered, our immediate gut impulse is to get away from the feeling because it is so unpleasant. So we impulsively turn to distracting behaviors that ultimately only serve to give fear control over our lives. We abandon ourselves in the process by dishonoring what it is we are feeling. Ironically, the distracting behaviors tend to get out of control and help us to believe that we are incompetent at functioning in the world. Acknowledging fear is required in order to respond to it in a healthy way.

We started working with Leila, a 40-year-old female lawyer, very "successful" in her career and very unsuccessful in a fourteen-year-long collaboration in fear that she called marriage. Her husband, struggling with his own avoidance of fear, moved out after he told her he was sick and tired of putting up with her rage and intense verbal attacks. Leila was shocked at Jim's "impulsive behavior" of leaving, which she described as extreme. When she started counseling, she insisted that Jim was experiencing midlife crisis. She wanted to spend her therapeutic dollar talking about how troubled he had always been and how she continually rescued him in their time together. She represented that she was not an attacking person and that Jim clearly did not appreciate how hard she had worked to make sure he was happy.

Leila was an adoption lawyer. She made a lot of money in this field but it cost her dearly in her emotional well-being. In the process of arranging adoptions, Leila would hear some very tragic stories around the circumstances of any particular baby's biological family of origin. She was overtly stoic about these devastating stories, but they were clearly taking their toll on her.

During the first three weeks of our relationship, Leila called us every other day. Usually clients call between appointments when they are in some type of emotional crisis. When we returned those early calls Leila would not tell us she was in crisis. She would act it out.... right in our direction. One time she called demanding that she needed to talk to one of us right away. She did not answer the phone when we returned her call. On the third try she was there and her question was, "Jim invited me to dinner tonight. Should I go?" We reminded her that these "between" calls lead us to the assumption that she was in crisis and that if she was feeling fearful about something she needed to talk about that. Another time she left two voice mails wanting to speak with one of us and upon our return call she pointedly asked, "Did Jim call you?" We asked why she did not ask Jim directly. We reiterated that when she called between sessions for help, she needed to be in touch with her feelings of terror and talk about that.

Soon thereafter, Leila left a message on our voice mail canceling all further appointments. When we called her back, she stated with remarkable hostility that she needed "shrinks who would be more soothing and comforting" to her. After one or two information questions she revealed that she'd had a very difficult weekend and she was afraid to call for help. She was ashamed and afraid to have and express her fear. After all, she was an all-powerful lawyer who performed miracles for people. She couldn't possibly need help in any way. Her impulse upon fear was to distract herself by going after people on a superficial level to make her feel better. This was fruitless because at these times she would withhold what it was she was really feeling anyway. Instead, she would behave in a pushy manner, which pushed people away. Moreover, her reaction to fear by getting aggressive got her the opposite of what it was she said she wanted — comfort. Jim was fed up with unkind treatment and quite frankly so were we.

When we explained to Leila what we observed about her behavior, we concluded that strong evidence existed that she was suffering from Vicarious Trauma. We believed she needed to look into that directly and if it didn't resonate for her we would be happy to refer her out for a better fit. We were very clear that we did not want to enable her in the continuing dance around her issues. At that point in our conversation, she emphatically had a change of heart and wanted an extra session that week.

Vicarious Trauma took its toll on Leila whereby she was re-creating a painful scenario from her past with the outcome of abandonment. Now that Leila was ready to get down to work, she revealed that she was raised as an only child in the swank Park Avenue section of New York City. Her father was a busy doctor who was rarely home and her mother was a very beautiful and very depressed former model who was overmedicating herself with lots of prescription drugs. Even though she was there physically, she really wasn't there emotionally. Leila was passed off to a series of nannies. Eventually her mother took it too far and died from a prescription medicine overdose. Leila's father never really dealt with the tragedy and indulged her to try keeping her happy. She shared that her favorite pastime as a child was reading the Little Madeline books, a series about a French orphan.

Leila's work was now traumatizing her by triggering an historical event where legitimate grief was deferred. Leila needed to have that grief but she felt afraid and out-of-control when it came to the surface of her consciousness. She'd lost her mother and felt abandoned and that terrible event needed to be honored.

*What she would come to know in her recovery is that the abandonment drama was always initiated with her own self-abandonment by dishonoring her feeling state when it was actually fear on board. Fear and subsequent **self**-abandonment is always the backdrop for re-creation of the impasse.*

Responding, rather than *reacting*, to emotional fear is the most important part of recovering from Vicarious Trauma. Responding is a discipline that requires much mental structure and practice in order to become efficient at it. Responding to fear is best developed by following three distinct behavioral steps: *STOP, LOOK, and LISTEN!* Do you remember this phrase being taught to you as a child when learning how to cross the street? It is a fitting analogy. Some streets are easier to cross than others. How many streets have you crossed when you never even bothered to **Stop, Look, and Listen**? At some of the dangerous intersections you could easily be mowed down if you didn't adhere to the rules. When you find yourself at a scary emotional intersection in your work, the rule of *responding* is to **Stop, Look, and Listen**.

Let's start with **Stop**. First, identify your personal red light. For some of us, our anger is our personal red light. When we feel afraid due to some *trauma content* we have heard on the job, our acting-out distraction from the feeling of fear may be anger. Perhaps something is going on in the client's story that triggers an historical fear or an early break to our spiritual perspective. We might typically become impatient, frustrated, irritated and angry. That is our red light. *STOP!* We are at a gap in the Spiritual Bridge, an impasse. Don't retreat back into the darkness of the ego and breathe more life into the fear.

Simply *STOP*. Be humble and realistic by accepting that sometimes it is easier to stop sooner than at other times. With practice we become better and better at stopping sooner – a much nicer way to treat ourselves.

Untreated Vicarious Trauma sets us up to distract ourselves from historical fear with various acting-in or acting-out behaviors. In these situations, we are invariably the ones who suffer most. Ironically, when the acting-out distraction is anger, we can find ourselves at a place where the problem of getting mad becomes the greatest reminder of our need to respond rather than react.

It doesn't take long to identify a personal stop light. Just make sure you never tell yourself, "I don't know" or "I'm trying" as you begin to develop this skill. These statements are two of the most popular distractions to avoid dealing with fear and serve as a profound form of self-abandonment that keeps us stuck in the victim position, widens the impasse and leaves us feeling powerless and hopeless. There is really no such thing as "trying" when we make choices for dealing with trauma. We are either doing it or not doing it. We don't have to be hard on ourselves when we are not doing it, but let's at least be honest about it. Being honest with ourselves unblocks the path of forward movement.

When we ask ourselves the hard questions about our acting-in or acting out distractions, the answer "I don't know" is only more denial of Vicarious Trauma and feeds into our struggle with the underlying theme of incompetence. It undermines our ability to respond to fear. Of course we know why, but if we copped to it we'd then take on the responsibility of being human like everyone else.

If you are afraid to look at "why", simply say so as a first step in rising above fear. Stop and honor your feeling of fear. It is okay and makes perfect sense that you would experience fear working with populations that tell us appalling stories.

We always know in our heart of hearts what's going on with us. Stuck in the ego, we tend to be afraid to **LOOK** at it. Once we have stopped the distracting behaviors, we have freed ourselves to look inward and reveal the truth in what is happening. **We are suffering from Vicarious Trauma.** We can then *listen* peacefully to our inner story and realize we deserve to relinquish judgment and to be more patient with ourselves and the traumatizing aspects of our work. The *listen* part is where we allow a thought of peace to enter our minds.

The enigma is that many of us try to overcome fear out of our egos, a system based in fear to begin with. For example, we might get very *intellectual* in our attempt to overcome fear. We go to conferences, take continuing education, preserve our credentials and keep current on our malpractice insurance. We have a wealth of education and information but consistently tend to not integrate the information in a way that affords us the opportunity to recognize our own level of work-related stress.

Another example – we focus physically. We work out regularly at the gym, become nutrition enthusiasts, take yoga and kick boxing. Yet, we still do not feel sound.

Another pattern – we tout the importance of emotional growth and spend exorbitant amounts of time with others so that they might become whole while we do nothing about our own emotional well-being.

When we cannot integrate what we know to be true into what we believe to be true, we are at that familiar impasse in the Spiritual Bridge suffering from our own trauma reaction. When we consciously exchange our purpose from *maintaining ourselves at the impasse* to *bridging to our higher consciousness* we can acknowledge our fear and separation anxiety because we are then empowered to do something about it. We can meet *discouraging feeling states* because we know what to do when we are in them. We give the feelings to our higher thinking and receive peace in return. Spiritual training can actually raise the baseline happiness set point of the brain. It can change the basic pattern of prefrontal activation in a way that elicits more positive emotion. This inner transition is then environmentally mirrored for us through a series of corrective and uplifting events.

Responding **to fear** is the exercise of free will for freedom from Vicarious Trauma. Freedom from absorbing the pain and suffering that our clients' stories tend to impose on themselves – and vicariously – on us. *Responding* rather than *reacting* brings with it the knowledge of our true higher purpose – to extend and receive love. Once we know our purpose we are ready to link up to our higher brain. We are worthy and ready to receive and offer love freely. Through this reciprocal process we perceive ourselves centered in the **present**. Here we heal from trauma and experience peace, creativity and joy.

STEP 5

Reconnecting to the Spirit
I AM

Reconnecting to the Spirit is receiving the power of the higher mind. Here is our moment of truth. Now we are ready to be who we truly are. Once you have moved through the first four steps you are ready to complete the exchange. You have relinquished judgment of yourselves. You have used thoughts of peace to let go of fear. You are now ready to move from the neural circuitry that runs through your limbic brain and to receive your higher self. This is the only step that mentally requires you to do absolutely nothing. Just be still. Simply be present for your higher thinking. Mending the Spiritual Bridge has opened the way. No longer invested in maintaining the false idols of historical grievances continually reinforced through Vicarious Trauma, and having moved beyond separation anxiety you are ready to receive the characteristics of the spiritual self. This requires no concerted effort on your part. It is the accepting portion of the exchange of purpose. These characteristics come naturally as you reconnect. At this point it is important to remember that a state of readiness to receive them is not the same as a state of *mastery* in receiving them. *Readiness* is the decision to receive these qualities as precious gifts delivered from your higher thinking. *Mastery* is embracing these attributes so that they become the core of your identity, which had become so disjointed through trauma. Repetition and practice in accepting these traits brings us to mastery of them. Readiness occurs as you remember your true identity – a good human – sometimes spiritually referred to as the **I Am**.

Reconnecting to the Spirit implies release of the past and response to fear, or the application of self-forgiveness. When we have exercised this enough times, forgiveness tends to come to mind quickly and doesn't require much concerted effort. Think about how much psychic energy we pour into fear-based distractions within ourselves and with others. If we gave a fraction of that energy to the discipline of connecting to the higher brain, our state of mind and our interactions would be far more centered and peaceful.

Those who spend little or no time bridging to the higher mind tend to complain that they have difficulty relating to a personal concept of a Higher Power. No wonder! They exert little or no energy in that inner relationship and then feel disappointed about it. A Higher Power doesn't travel the Drama Triangle. We are not victims waiting to be rescued. Furthermore, why do we receive something so great so infrequently? It makes sense that with the chronic stress in our jobs compared to what we get in bridging, we would be bridging all the time. Bridging to the **I Am** or building a relationship with the higher thinking needs our input. M. Scott Peck wrote in <u>The Road Less Traveled</u> that in building a loving relationship, many times quantity is quality time. Devote some time to your spiritual self. You are worthy of it.

How you practice mastery in reconnecting is a very personal and individualized practice. You will create bridging exercises that work for you. Religion, or a particular style of expressing faith in a Higher Power is only one form of practicing mastery.

We have gathered a partial list of bridging exercises that may help you create your own path.

- Meditation
- Practice yoga
- Be in nature
- Engage in the arts
- Pray for someone
- Read and journal
- Cook a meal for someone
- Star gaze
- Help the sick
- Attend someone else's church or temple
- Exercise
- Do charitable acts
- Take care of children
- Play games
- Help the elderly
- Teach
- Read for the blind
- Participate in an ecological endeavor
- Join or form a spiritual study and/or encouragement group
- Give compliments
- Listen actively
- Pay attention
- Express gratitude
- Be present

When we are peaceful in our minds, we receive the energy of the **I Am**. This energy gives us characteristics of trust, honesty, tolerance, gentleness, joy, self-intimacy, generosity, patience, faithfulness and open-mindedness. First, we utilize these characteristics unto ourselves. This feels so wonderfully liberating and powerful that we are enthusiastic to extend the same onto others. We then co-create spiritual alliances.

Trust is the first characteristic we receive as we let our minds be still. Having moved through the first four steps, we have trust in ourselves as we remove the "Under Construction" sign that earlier stood at the impasse. We can let go of the illusion of control and self-judgment that kept us in denial about our own legitimate, work-related misery. Our minds are peaceful and we trust that is all that is necessary to receive the healing power of the spiritual perspective.

Self-honesty is the essence of the **I Am**. Honesty can be described as consistency and signifies the elimination of inner conflict due to what once was a need to distract ourselves from the affliction of trauma. It marks the end of self-deception or denial. It proclaims our self-acceptance and opens the way back to our true identities. Reconnecting to higher thinking also keeps us honest with ourselves when tempted to stray off the path of recovery and is the motivation that reminds us to remember the first four steps when we meet up with separation anxiety.

Self-tolerance is the result of the relinquishment of self-judgment. We now understand that we are *not* perfect, we cannot compete with "God" by performing miracles, and that we are human just like everyone else. Honesty helps us notice that we will make errors and going into shame about it only furthers our trauma. Self-tolerance protects us from going into that shame attack when we have made a mistake. Noticing that an error has been made now comes from an unspoiled awareness, not from a position of judgment and fear. Free from shame, we can give the error over to our higher brain and thereby invite wisdom in to handle the problem. Tolerance helps us remember that we are worthy to receive a personal sense of God because we are not separate. Therefore, we maintain a position of being self-accepting and letting infinite wisdom resolve the daily challenges of hearing *trauma content* through our work.

Gentleness can be described as the inability to do harm to oneself or anyone else. When we live gently with ourselves, we make a conscious decision to not berate ourselves for our professional or personal struggles. Berating oneself furthers the negative force of any trauma narrative. Self-harm is only an issue when one is invested in holding onto judgment as a way to stay separate and be "true" to an insane belief that we are not worthy of connecting to our higher consciousness. Gentleness is strength and spirituality and does not imply the worldly connotation of passivity or numbness.

Joy is the awareness and appreciation of the goodness and the beauty in you – something we are highly at risk to lose sight of when we suffer from Vicarious Trauma. It is the state we achieve when we are honest, tolerant and gentle. Joy is different from the feeling called "glad" or "happy" – the feeling that results from happenstance or some pleasing outside event. Joy is the resulting state of the most precious inside event – a state of release that is free of fear, shame and anger. As we receive joy, we begin to pay attention to our wonder rather than our woe. When we have met and risen above our separation anxiety, joy is what we experience in its place – a very powerful place to be.

Self-intimacy is experienced as a result of defenselessness. Fear nullified, defenses no longer serve a purpose. We are free of the need to protect ourselves from the context of a painful past, set up again and again through listening to the trauma stories of others. Defensiveness is what kept our Vicarious Trauma symptoms as the altars at which we worshiped. As we receive intimacy, we state, "I could discover nothing about myself that would make me unlovable to myself." Self-intimacy is the characteristic that compels us to extend Love to others. It is the mainstay of a spiritual alliance – so important in helping others heal.

Generosity with ourselves is received as we reconnect. This is not the fear-based characteristic of greed. Greed is the result of being separated from goodness in us. Greed is a distraction based in thoughts of lack and scarcity. When we are separate, perceiving ourselves as alone, we believe we have nothing and so compensate by keeping things for ourselves. Generosity with oneself signifies the quality of quantity time connecting to the higher mind. Being generous with ourselves means receiving the abundance of peace in us as much as we can. Ironically, when this generosity is received we are driven to give it away to others. Generosity is the main dynamic that ensures we stay the path of spiritual connection.

Patience with ourselves is received in the **I Am**. Since being in the present is the human experience of eternity, there are no time constraints, and therefore, no need for impatience. No longer separate, we release the need to control things based on being the only person to do the job. Since we give away control based in fear, we gain patience within and set healthier boundaries for ourselves and with others. Passion is the root word of patience and we begin to feel that passion again in our work. Patience gives us clear inner vision. When we use inner vision to perceive any particular event we have faith that the event serves us by either protecting us or providing us with some new self-understanding. We have faith that we will be spiritually served by the event even if it doesn't appear that way in its original traumatizing manifestation.

Open-mindedness occurs as we receive the power of higher thinking, and with it we are empowered to take risks, extend ourselves and realize the talents and abilities we possess on a grand scale. We begin to see with a vision that is not limited to our eyes and we begin to believe that there are no limits to the possibilities. As we accept this vision for ourselves we see the endless possibilities for others. Creativity soars, enthusiasm resounds and courage abounds. It is the open mind that has the power to view healing as an event that occurs but never from an ego-driven need to control.

It is important to differentiate between embracing these characteristics and acting them out. There are some who get into what we call a case of the tail wagging the dog. They think that if they *act* patient, tolerant, and so on, then that will be acceptable. This is not how it works. When we are out of denial about our own trauma reactions, in release of the past and responding to fear, we are centered in the present and able to receive these spiritual gifts. We do not act them out – we become them.

When work's traumatizing challenges harm us, impair us, or trigger our own historical upsets, we can remember forgiveness (relinquishment of judgment followed with a thought of peace) quite easily with a mended Spiritual Bridge. Connection to higher thinking or the spiritual perspective empowers us to stay centered and trustworthy of our ability to cope with the certainty of the Vicarious Trauma we experience through helping others.

CHAPTER NINE

Organizations as Vicarious Trauma Cauldrons

As we gathered stories and testimonials from *helping* professionals during the creation of this book, one common theme became obvious – that they are terrified to discuss their trauma. The only way they were willing to share their stories was with our promise to maintain their anonymity. As reported by Wilson and Thomas, even though it is so obvious that Vicarious Trauma is an occupational hazard, over 79.9% of surveyed *helpers* reported having difficulty discussing their exposure to Vicarious Trauma, 75% felt alienated from their peers, 73% felt a lack of support from their licensing boards and professional organizations, and over 62% felt reluctant to speak honestly about Vicarious Trauma at all. (Wilson & Thomas, 2004)

When professionals were asked why they believe they are susceptible to Vicarious Trauma, these were their responses, as cited in the 1998 Second Annual Poster Session for organizational coping strategies:

- lack of experience with trauma victims;
- caseloads too high with trauma victims;
- hearing repetitive stories of trauma or abuse;
- working with clients who re-enact pathological relationships in therapy or in the *helping* relationship itself;
- working without adequate support or supervision;
- fear of asking for help due to being seen as incompetent;
- experiencing a traumatic event with a client such as an attempted suicide, or suicide, or other severe psychiatric break from reality;
- working with clients in a work context in which concrete signs of success are few;
- empathizing with client's experiences of severe pain in their lives and not being able to hold to strong boundaries;

- unable to maintain a professional distance consistent with the ethical standards outlined by the professional boards (McSwain, K, Robinson, R., & Panteluk, L, 1998).

One therapist reported the following incident that remains with her to this day:

> *"I was seeing a client who admitted he had a serious addiction to prescription drugs and had committed to go for treatment. His consumption was so profuse that I had no idea how he drove a car or functioned in his high level professional career. One day, he came for therapy and brought his 7-year-old daughter who waited in my waiting room. How he drove to my office that day with his daughter in the car was appalling to me. During the session it became apparent that he was highly debilitated and as he spoke, he began to lose consciousness. I was in a serious dilemma. His child was in the waiting room counting on her father to take her to ballet following the session. The father was passed out on my couch unable to function at even the most minimal level let alone drive this child in a car. It was obvious that another adult had to be called to assist with this situation. Yet, the child would certainly be traumatized when another adult or emergency vehicle arrived to take care of her father in this extremely diminished capacity. As I quickly made a professional decision to call an emergency responder I had to compress my own trauma response and make emergency decisions for an incapacitated person where the liability could potentially have been overwhelming. I then had to provide guidance and support for his young child who was not my client and appeared to be in a state of absolute panic as I approached her in the waiting room."*

Janine, Clinical Social Worker

Another therapist wrote the following:

> *"Although I worked in an office with three other therapists, we were individual practitioners and so, had very little professional interaction in the course of a work day. Never before did I feel the estrangement from my peers than when I had an overwhelming event take place in my office. A client who had been released two days prior from an in-patient program came to see me for an intake session. She filled out her forms and began to share with me her path of recovery from a lifetime of physical and sexual abuse. When I asked her about medication she recited a laundry list of ingredients that made up one heck of*

a psychotropic cocktail. As she began to share her history her eyes rolled back into her head and she stiffened up in the chair. I called her name three or four times before I realized that this client had gone catatonic before my eyes. No amount of talking, calling or even raising my voice could move her from this paralyzed state. I went to the intake form and called the emergency number. It was a non-working number. I ran to offices of my peers, knocked on two of three office doors asking for some help and guidance. Instead, I received an absolute resistance to becoming involved. In fact, the best response I got was a blank stare from someone with whom I had worked for many years. Feeling helpless, inadequate and at fault, I finally dialed 9-1-1. What really struck me as dysfunctional was my numbing to the point that much of my concern was around keeping my next client waiting."

Donald, Psychologist

We must be able to identify Vicarious Trauma without shame or fear of reprisal. As professionals we need to recognize that Vicarious Trauma is a veritable occupational hazard. We must accept *helpers'* reactions as expected and normal responses and provide a safe environment for debriefing and healing.

Over time if we have not adapted to the trauma stories we have heard, our entire psychological, biological and spiritual system begins to wear down and malfunction. You will recognize system failure when you are inadequately responding to the *trauma content*. We need to be aware of the length, duration and intensity of our exposure, the type of clients involved, especially if they are suicidal or children, and our own trauma histories. Additionally, organizational factors worsen Vicarious Trauma by overworking staff and providing insufficient staffing, supervision and consultation. This needs to be addressed immediately so that those in the *helping* professions can continue to provide a much needed service to the community.

In order to prevent Vicarious Trauma, organizations can advocate for the continued strength of the stated ethical principles and guidelines of their professions for their licensees, group members, employees and/or staff through social support, group cohesion, training, and trauma-informed staffing supervision and consultation (McSwain *et al*, 1998) Professionals at all levels – Board level, management, and in the trenches – all must be informed about the risks of not addressing this silent killer that leads to a community of traumatized heroes. Everyone must be encouraged to address this problem so they can maintain the strong ethical principles of autonomy, beneficence, non-malfeasance and justice. If left untreated, Vicarious Trauma can become emotionally contagious, with numbing, hypervigilance, irritability, indifference, cynicism, hopelessness and despair spreading rampant amongst the ranks of *helpers*.

Appropriate staff or professional training for the prevention of Vicarious Trauma includes the following essential pieces:

- recognition that Vicarious Trauma is an occupational hazard and is de-stigmatized within the organization or practice group;
- honoring and respecting one another as human beings as well as *helping* professionals;
- supporting wellness by providing adequate vacation time, sick time and personal leave;
- building a culture of excellence;
- providing adequate pay and benefits;
- rewarding clinical skills;
- setting positive goals;
- building up buffering strategies;
- always backing up your team;
- creating a safe learning community; encouraging and rewarding continuing education;
- obtaining consultation for yourselves as administrators, managers and supervisors;
- being confidential and never penalizing someone for revealing Vicarious Trauma;
- training competent supervisors who have an understanding of the dynamics of Vicarious Trauma;
- requiring supervision to prevent the contagion that Vicarious Trauma can perpetrate upon a healthy organization (International Trauma Consultants, 2006).

Organizations need to provide adequate supervision for the critical *helping* structure inherent in every healing relationship that includes:

- A safe, nurturing environment with clear and appropriate role boundaries in which the client's affect and the *helper's* empathic strain are both successfully and individually managed.

- Conscious attention paid to the non-verbal piece of the relationship, the right-brain reaction, such as feelings, memories, and autonomic body responses such as increased heart and breathing rate so that *helpers* can be aware of and manage effectively the reactions they are experiencing.

- A heightened awareness of the levels of countertransference that are occurring must be taken into account, i.e. the client and *helper* countertransference, the *helper* and the administrative body countertransfercnce, the colleague to colleague countertransference and the *helper* to the licensing board or governing body countertransference.

- Maintaining components of Vicarious Trauma supervision: awareness of Vicarious Trauma as a real problem, theoretical understanding of Vicarious Trauma, an understanding of childhood development, an ability to focus on the conscious and unconscious aspects of the *helping* relationship, creating a safe, private and confidential interpersonal climate with *helpers* so they can process their Vicarious Trauma without shame or fear of judgment, being educated in Vicarious Trauma and be attuned to the *helper's* condition or state (Wilson & Lindy, 2004).

A *helping* organization that pays strict attention to the prevention and healing of Vicarious Trauma will glean positive results, including healthy transformation of the client, healthy transformation of the *helper* as a professional and healthy transformation of the *helping* professional as a person. If the organization is doing its job, then this is the ultimate end result.

Here is a cogent case study presented by Doug, a psychologist/custody evaluator. Doug functioned in a therapeutic private practice in addition to performing custody evaluations for the Court in litigated divorce cases. In his jurisdiction, custody cases were either assigned by the judge in the Family Court or evaluators were selected by the divorcing couples. Here is what he wrote:

> *"I have a very active private practice and was invited by several lawyers and judges I knew to participate in the custody evaluator program in my state. To qualify, I took all the necessary training to become eligible through the court system to perform custody evaluations. In my private practice I focused my expertise on divorcing couples and children of divorce. I also enjoyed working with blended families and believed I had the expertise to work with the scope of family law. The court system was overloaded with divorce cases requiring custody evaluations and so I was busy as soon as I was added to the list of evaluators. The case I most remember that caused me the most anxiety involved two teenage girls, an undiagnosed bipolar mother, and a passive, but caring father. It was not my job to diagnose either party, but to determine where the children's best interests would be served in their living arrangements. I followed*

the protocols to the letter. I interviewed both parents and all collaterals. I had the children seen by an independent, neutral child specialist, selected by the parents, so I had additional information with which to make my recommendations. The mother was actually a very sad case. She so wanted to function as a good parent, but was emotionally out-of-control and was psychologically injurious to her children with her mood swings including outbursts of rage. The father was unsophisticated and worked a blue collar job while making every possible effort to meet the needs of two adolescent girls and their sports schedules. The mother disappeared for weeks at a time and the girls were definitive in wanting supervised visits with mom. The majority of custodial time with dad was assessed as appropriate.

One afternoon, I received thirteen angry and hysterical phone calls from Mom threatening to sue me and file a complaint with my board if I did not provide her equal access to the children. All these calls were documented. The recommendation, ultimately adopted by the court, was made to the court to place the girls with their father and to provide supervised visitation for the mother. Several weeks passed with no harassing phone calls or further contact with this family. I was working way too hard, in excess of sixty hours a week, with a huge caseload of custody evaluations. Two months later, I received a board complaint from the bipolar Mom. She alleged that I was prejudiced against her, that I did not follow the protocols, that I did not interview her family, and that the child specialist selected in the case was a personal friend of mine, who I influenced to select her ex-husband as primary custodian. I was freaked out for two years until this came before the board. I went through my files, line by line, searching for anything that could lead to such an upsetting turn in the road. I found nothing. I sent all my records to the board and waited. After six months I contacted a representative of my state board to see how the case was progressing and if they needed anything further from me. I was passed from person to person on the phone, each interaction proving fruitless in the way of getting any help. The only information I could get was that they were behind in addressing board complaints and would get back to me. The complaint itself was not as traumatizing as the treatment I received from my board. There was no one there willing to assist me either with procedure or with information regarding the case. Another year went by and finally I received notice of a hearing. Once again, I contacted my board to find out what I could expect. Did I need to call witnesses? Did I need a lawyer to represent me? Was my accuser being represented by counsel? Was the board going to protect my flawless record? No response at all! They used and abused me and when I needed them they aban-

doned me. I hired a lawyer to attend the hearing with me and within minutes the charges were dismissed. It was also traumatizing and heartbreaking to see the mom in so much pain and so disturbed as she acted out at the hearing. It was obvious that she suffered from mental illness. But what was more disturbing was the lack of interaction, or support, or connection from the Board. I thought that that was my board and I was astounded at the lack of compassion about my set of circumstances. I eventually withdrew from the court roster and now only practice in a more collaborative model. As an aside, four years later, the mom called to apologize for filing the complaint to the board. She had finally sought treatment for her bipolar disorder and was now on appropriate medication. She realized that the decisions made at the time where, in fact, in the best interest of her children."

Doug, Custodial Evaluator

Helpers who work in organizational settings need to be able to talk about their feelings with colleagues who will not judge them. Organizations need to support their staff in the practice of effective interoffice communication skills that help workers communicate with people at every level of the organization. It must be remembered that in many of these settings, caring for traumatized clients is a regular event, not an occasional occurrence. Therefore, exposure to trauma is frequent. Organizations need to offer balancing activities to their staff which includes honoring each other as heroes who do some of the hardest and most important work for people in the world.

It is noteworthy that many ethical codes do not mention the welfare of their professional members when discussing Second-Hand Shock Syndrome (Compassion Fatigue, Secondary Traumatic Stress Disorder and Vicarious Trauma). Quite the contrary! The welfare of *helpers* for their own sake is increasing in ethical importance. "Self-care" implies that the individual is responsible for preventing the problem and that it is the *helper's* problem when it does occur. There is only so much one can achieve without a shift in the environment in which one operates. Professional organizations need to move to make an effort to support the professionals in their battle against Vicarious Trauma. The *helping* professions need to expand their views to include professional welfare as an integral aspect of professional standards. This approach maintains and strengthens the clear and good judgment of the client. The client is well served but not at the expense or sacrifice of the *helper*.

Second-Hand Shock

CONCLUSION

If you are wondering at this point if you are suffering from Vicarious Trauma – good! We've accomplished our goal! Suffering in silence only makes the situation worse and reinforces the unhealthy shame that is associated with this normal stress response. We hope that you understand that Vicarious Trauma not only affects your mind – it literally alters the structure of your brain in a counter-productive fashion. It takes time and patience to repair the damage and it takes courage to examine yourself introspectively.

We encourage you to reach out to others who, through the reading of this book, you know are suffering. It is so important for *helpers* to rally together to de-stigmatize the inevitability of Vicarious Trauma. Now is your opportunity to consider the Miracle Worker Reverie, detach from it, and give yourself permission to ask for help.

By reading this book, you have been enlightened and have opened an important door for yourself and for the *helping* professions. The AFTERSHOCK Workbook will further you on this important journey through various contemplative and inter-active exercises. We encourage you to form Vicarious Trauma groups for collegiality, discussion and workbook guidance. Look to create a safe haven for yourself and your colleagues.

The call to help others is precious. You can preserve the integrity of the *helping* relationship by taking excellent care of yourself. We wish you well on your journey and we thank you for being our heroes.

PROFESSIONAL GROUP DISCUSSION QUESTIONS

The following are some group discussion questions. These questions are meant to generate meaningful interaction and to enhance comfort levels in dialoging about Vicarious Trauma.

1. What happens to our population if our *helpers* don't get treatment for Vicarious Trauma?

2. How can consumers recognize Vicarious Trauma symptoms in a professional they hire and what should they do?

3. How do we tell a colleague that we think he/she has Vicarious Trauma?

4. How do we recognize our own Vicarious Trauma?

5. What is the first step we need to take to help solve this problem?

6. How are our personal relationships affected by our Vicarious Trauma?

7. What are we afraid of?

8. If there was one thing we could do for ourselves to combat this problem, what would it be?

9. If we were at the board level or the managing partner of a law firm, what would we do with this knowledge after reading this book?

10. As consumers, how can we support our heroes in the battle against Vicarious Trauma?

11. Are the physical manifestations of Vicarious Trauma reversible?

12. As a professional, what do you do about the ethical violations you know you've made because you were suffering with Vicarious Trauma? How do you make amends?

13. Where does a professional go to receive treatment for Vicarious Trauma?

Contact us at **Vicarious Trauma Institute, www.vicarioustrauma.com** or **(480) 991-4119** for information about treatment options including individual weekly consultations, a three-day intensive treatment program, or a one-day in-service for your organization.

We hope you will complete the AFTERSHOCK Workbook in the second half of this book.

THE AFTERSHOCK WORKBOOK

Ellie Izzo, PhD, LPC

and

Vicki Carpel Miller, BSN, MS, LMFT

The Rapid Advance Process outlined in this workbook for addressing Vicarious Trauma is in no way a substitute for ongoing medical or psychiatric consultation, medication, individual, family, marital or group therapy, counseling or any other form of treatment for emotional disorders. We strongly urge our readers to seek out professional consultation for the treatment of their Vicarious Trauma.

CHAPTER 1

Introduction

We have been in the helping professions collectively for over 50 years. We have suffered and seen colleagues suffer from the effects of untreated Vicarious Trauma. Unfortunately, most of us believe we have to suffer in silence. Only recently has it been a little bit more acceptable to admit we may be compromised due to the stresses of our work. **Second-Hand Shock: Surviving & Overcoming Vicarious Trauma** and **The AFTERSHOCK Workbook** have been created to acknowledge and address this underreported professional epidemic in a respectful, compassionate and accepting manner. We want to bring what has been considered a secretive and highly sensitive subject out in the open so our heroes can secure the support, regard and assistance they so profoundly deserve. The price the *helper* pays, if Vicarious Trauma is left untreated, is excessive.

What is Vicarious Trauma? The technical definition of Vicarious Trauma is a transformation in the *helper*'s inner sense of identity and existence that results from utilizing controlled empathy when listening to clients' traumatic stories. More simply put Vicarious Trauma is a set of cognitive, emotional, physical and spiritual disturbances that result from helping trauma survivors. Every time *helper*s interact with clients, they are putting themselves at risk. Vicarious Trauma is nothing we deserve to feel ashamed of; it is a natural stress response to the difficult work we want to do well.

This workbook is designed to be used after reading Part 1 of **Second-Hand Shock: Surviving & Overcoming Vicarious Trauma**, an educational resource for all people in the *helping* professions or any lay person who is an active listener. We strongly suggest that you read **Second-Hand Shock: Surviving & Overcoming Vicarious Trauma** before attempting this workbook. In conjunction with the exercises, you will need a journal to work. As you proceed with this workbook, take your time and utilize this guide in a way that will best serve your individual needs.

CHAPTER 2

Do I Have Vicarious Trauma?

Assessing Vicarious Trauma takes some introspection and contemplation. Many of its associated symptoms are attributed to different causes, real or imagined. It will take time for you to identify and categorize them in a pattern that helps you to understand that you may be suffering from Vicarious Trauma.

At first, you may think you can not relate to some of the following questions. However, take time to consider them and reach deep within yourself to come up with an answer. Many people are in denial about having Vicarious Trauma because there is so much stigma and punitive action attached to having it. *Helper*s are resistant to consider the possibility that it is happening to them, so they suffer in silence. Sadly, many *helper*s also close off their own personal histories. They stuff them away because they are too painful to recall or to address. Yet, an awareness of one's history is absolutely necessary in the prevention and treatment of Vicarious Trauma. Instead, we choose distracting behaviors that inevitably fail us miserably. If you are working in a *helping* profession, or if you are simply a good friend or an active listener, this set of qualifying questions may likely lead you to complete this workbook.*

*Acknowledgement and thanks go to Karen Saakvitne and Laurie Anne Pearlman for their workbook, Transforming the Pain: A Workbook on Vicarious Traumatization for *Helping* Professionals Who Work with Traumatized Clients, (NY: Norton Publishing 1996).

EVALUATION QUESTIONS
Get Analytical About the Type of Work That You Do

Sometimes we get lost in the minutia of our jobs and lose sight of the bigger picture. Take some time here to look at the nature of your work from the outside looking in.

What do you do for a living? _____

_____

_____

Are you in a *helping* capacity in your work?_____

How many hours per week do you engage in your professional focus? _____

Do you work more than 25 hours directly listening to people's stories each week?

_____

Do you work with difficult clients? _____

Do you perceive you can exercise options about the people you work with? _____

Do you have a break during the day for personal time? _____ If so, what do you do?

_____

_____

Do you have adequate staffing or supervision?_____

Who are the clients you feel most challenged with and why? _____

_____

_____

Do you feel adequately trained to perform your work functions?_____

Is your training appropriate for your work? _____

Looking at Yourself as a Professional

Sometimes the boundary between who we are and what we do becomes blurred. Take a moment here to remember your professional identity as a part of who you are.

Do you enjoy your work? What do you like most? What do you like least?_____

_____

_____

_____

Do you see yourself as respected in your field? _____

Are you financially well compensated for your work? _____

Do you feel you provide value to the clients you work with? _____

Is your motivation and desire to be in your field the same as when you began this work?

_____

_____

Do you work in fear of making a mistake for which you will be punished? _____

Describe your professional style. _____

_____

_____

Has a client ever frightened you? _____

_____

What are some of the evaluations made by your clients about you that have been disturbing? _____

_____

_____

Has anyone ever written you a complaint letter? What did they say? _____

_____

_____

_____

Has anyone ever filed a formal complaint about you to your licensing board or other

authority? _____ If so, what was the complaint? _____

_____

_____

What aspects of your work concern you? _____

Do you feel safe in your work? _____ If your answer is no, in what areas do you

feel at risk? _____

_____

_____

Do you have anyone to talk to about your fears at work; someone with whom you can

be totally and completely honest? _____

Looking at Yourself as a Person

This part of the workbook offers you the opportunity for introspection. This is your
chance to be honest with yourself about some of the challenges you may face, just like
any other human being.

Do you feel emotionally equipped to handle the distress of your clients? _____

Do you have a personal trauma history?_____

Has your sense of being connected to a higher order of things changed? Do you feel

your spirit is broken? _____

Has your world view changed? _____

Do you recognize your strong feeling states? _____

Are you feeling satisfied with your family connections?_____

Are you suffering with any chronic or intermittent unexplained physical symptoms?

_____

Are you sleeping well?_____

Do you worry? _____

Are you happy? _____

Do you make time for your own personal enjoyment?_____

What do you do to relax?_____

_____

_____

Do you believe you have intimacy in your relationships? _____

Do you exercise?_____

Do you perceive yourself as being safe in the world? _____

EXERCISE:

An Act of Courage

Write down five symptoms you have identified through this assessment that you think may be symptoms of Vicarious Trauma.

1. _____

2. _____

3. _____

4. _____

5. _____

EXERCISE:

An Act of Faith

Write down five things that would be different and better for you if you allowed yourself to heal from the reality of Vicarious Trauma:

1. _____

2. _____

3. _____

4. _____

5. _____

Now you have begun your journey. You have started to courageously explore and assess aspects of your work and your personal history that may contribute to your vulnerability to vicarious trauma. It is important that you now take this new consciousness to the next level.

The reality of Vicarious Trauma is nothing to be ashamed of. It is certainly no surprise that professional *helper*s would fall prey to this insidious syndrome. Be accepting of your struggle and make a commitment to move forward and address this painful issue.

CHAPTER 3

Rapid Advance Process

Since Vicarious Trauma is experienced as a painful inner transformation in an individual's identity, it makes sense that the greatest negative impact can be described as a break to the essence or the spirit of the individual. After internalizing trauma content stories over time through the strain of controlled empathy, it should not be surprising that our heroes can find themselves poor or broken in spirit. The core spiritual identity, the basic essence of the *helper* becomes nearly inaccessible.

The spirit of *helping* individuals can be identified as that level of consciousness that rises above upset and stress and responds to negative situations with dynamics such as courage, faith, hope, trust and forgiveness. The neurocircuitry of trauma makes it very challenging to access the higher brain without a conscious and concerted effort. When people are in a state of disconnect from this powerful higher perspective, they are left with lower, limbic brain reactions such as fear and anxiety as their primary context for perceiving the world. They become stuck in self-definition that is pessimistic and judgmental.

In addition, the experience of the **Miracle Worker Reverie**, discussed in Chapter 7, in *Second-Hand Shock: Surviving & Overcoming Vicarious Trauma*, puts *helping* professionals in a position that is diametrically opposed to a healthy spiritual connection. The Reverie has *helpers* almost competing with their own value system, morals and ethics, rather than connecting with a healthy perception of their higher self.

Vicarious Trauma leaves individuals at great risk to be in separation from the spiritual perspective or their higher thinking. An individual's sense of spiritual identity, a very personal and individualized experience, is free from self-judgment. Vicarious Trauma puts the *helper* in the position of self-regard that attacks one's fundamental nature and states: "I am powerless; I am depressed;" or the opposite, "I am omnipotent and I am god-like."

Treatment must include a viable method for bridging or reconnecting to the higher mind so the *helper* can remain peaceful, healthy, centered, open, neutral, and positive in their work. Vicarious Trauma precipitates an impasse in the *helper*'s Spiritual Bridge or neural pathways to that higher level of consciousness. Recovery from Vicarious Trauma must include some way to mend that impasse and restore the neural pathways to the higher left brain or the spiritual point of view.

Before we embark on this journey of recovery, first clear your mind of any negative or counterproductive notions of spirituality. Many of us were raised with religious dogma and practices that were either heavy handed or punitive in their orientation. Others were raised with no spiritual practice at all. Some of us have simply allowed that part of our experience to atrophy over time.

EXERCISE:

Spirituality

Please list below any negative connotations that the word 'spirituality' elicits for you.

_____

_____

_____

_____

_____

_____

_____

_____

_____

_____

EXERCISE:

Characteristics, Traits and Behaviors

Make a list of the traits, characteristics, and behaviors you would like to create as you reconnect to your higher mind (For example, patience, peacefulness, absence of worry, tolerance, hope, joy). _____

_____

_____

_____

_____

What would that part of you feel like? _____

_____

_____

_____

_____

How would that part be of assistance to you when you feel troubled? Please do not rush through this segment. _____

_____

_____

_____

_____

_____

You are now ready to proceed with the Rapid Advance Process. By completing the five steps, you will have the opportunity to mend, build and strengthen strong neural pathways to your higher brain. In so doing, you will have the opportunity to develop a reliable practice of accessing your own remarkable internal resources for dealing with the stresses of your work and the resulting anguish or numbness of Vicarious Trauma.

The Rapid Advance Process consists of five steps for Vicarious Trauma recovery:

Step 1. Reveal the History

Step 2. Recognize the Impasse

Step 3. Release the Past

Step 4. Respond to Fear

Step 5. Reconnect with the Spirit

Please remember this is not a substitute for treatment for recovered memories of traumatizing events earlier in one's life. This Process is for victims of Vicarious Trauma. If you are an adult survivor of serious <u>untreated</u> childhood trauma, we caution you about engaging in a *helping* profession without first receiving appropriate treatment for your psychological injuries. To do so would compromise your effectiveness and objectivity as a *helping* professional.

Come along with us as we take Daniel, a family lawyer, through the five steps of the Rapid Advance Process. Accompanying him on his journey will help you to focus on applying the steps for yourself. First, let us introduce you to him.

Daniel: A Case Study

Daniel was referred for treatment by his primary care physician, following an annual physical. He had met with his doctor due to multiple physical annoyances. When his doctor found nothing medically wrong, he suggested that Daniel might be experiencing physical symptoms due to psychological stress and referred him to us.

Daniel presented as a man sophisticated in many dimensions. He was well dressed, well spoken, confident, calm and charming and really didn't understand why he was referred for a Vicarious Trauma consultation. Daniel's success as a family lawyer had its benefits and its disadvantages. While he was very conscious of all the benefits he had enjoyed from a thriving practice, he was less conscious of how the stress in his work affected his psyche. After some interaction with him about the definition of Vicarious Trauma and after asking him the assessment questions, he experienced an "aha" moment. He was visibly concerned with how he had unwittingly been traumatized through the nature of his work.

Daniel was married for over 20 years and had 3 teenage boys. He reported he worked over 60 hours a week as a family lawyer and that he was extremely successful financially. He stated that his work took its toll on him, but that the financial rewards were worth the effort. He had provided a lavish life style for his family and wanted to keep it that way.

He shared that he was involved in a case where he was spending long hours and worrying excessively. After worrying for a couple of weeks, he started developing headaches and digestive problems. "This case is taking years off my life." he said. We asked him to elaborate. He told the tale of a client seeking a divorce with young children. This father of three wanted joint custody of his children and was working two jobs and juggling time so he could parent his kids. The wife, according to his client, was vindictive and angry because he had left the relationship, and most recently, she had made allegations that he was sexually inappropriate with the middle son. The client vehemently denied the behavior and asked Daniel to help him gain custody of the children.

Daniel related an unusually high stress level around this particular case, and stated that he felt overwhelmed when working on it at his office. He felt estranged from his family and toiled late nights and weekends just to catch up. He said his wife complained about his late hours and lack of time spent with her and the boys. He admitted he was unable to attend the sporting events his children participated in due to his heavy court and client schedules. This, he said, he regretted more than anything. He loved his boys and his wife, but his work was too important financially to the family. There was no time for connection right now. Work came first and he didn't have much interest in anything else. He himself was curious about his obsessive nature when it came to the facts of this one particular case. He was having unmanageable anxiety around the allegations lodged against his client. This was a case he wanted desperately to win.

STEP ONE

Reveal Your History

IT WAS

You may think that your history holds no triggers or no truly upsetting events. Nonetheless, the hippocampus of your brain regulates every memory you ever experienced. While there is a high percentage of *helping* professionals who are trauma survivors, there are an equal number who are not. Whether your fears from childhood are a dark closet, being accosted by a scary child, being caught in the rain, coming home from school and having no one in the house, hearing strange noises, having nightmares, losing a friend, losing a love, accidents, feeling publicly embarrassed in school or in front of the family, becoming ill and missing out on important activities, surgery, hospital stays, shyness in school, moving, just to name a few – they are stored. These historical feeling states can be triggered repetitively through listening to the trauma content of your clients. An awareness of your historical hot buttons is crucial in the maintenance of your emotional and spiritual well being in your work.

Here is Daniel's story for Revealing the History. Hopefully, it will stimulate your thoughts about your own childhood experiences.

Revealing the History: Daniel

Daniel was born in the Midwest and was brought up by loving parents. He was the older of two children, with a sister five years younger. She looked up to her big brother as if he were her hero. Daniel stated he and his sister grew up in excellent health. He said his childhood was idyllic and that nothing was remarkable.

We first asked him to describe his parents as he could remember them from a very young age. The five words he used to describe his father were passive, deferring, compliant, good provider and absent. He related that his father was passive and deferred in most instances to his mother. If something was important to his father, he would speak up. Otherwise, he was fairly taciturn. He didn't bond strongly with his father, who worked many hours in order to provide financial security for the family.

The five words he used to describe his mother were strong, caring, strict, perfectionistic and nurturing. He also added that his mother was extremely socially conscious and her reputation in the community was a very important part of her identity. He described his parents as affectionate and caring toward each other. If there was any conflict, it was handled behind closed doors.

Daniel described himself as an over-achieving child whose primary purpose was to be an excellent reflection of his family. He excelled in school, was on the debate team, played tennis, and was accepted to an Ivy League college. He was rarely disciplined as a child since he rarely made any mistakes. Daniel was raised in the Jewish faith, attended religious education, attained his Bar Mitzvah, and celebrated high holy days and other holidays with his nuclear and extended family.

His family went through a difficult time at around age 14 when Daniel's father lost his business. Money was tight, his father was emotionally tighter and his mother was scared. This situation resolved about a year later when Daniel's father obtained other suitable employment. During the financial crisis, he recalls his father going through the house turning off all the lights and stating, "What do you think....we own the electric company?" Daniel learned during that time to study in his room with a flash-light. He was relieved when this period was over.

The family spent quality time together going to amusement parks, the zoo, playing games together, attending theatre, movies, the children's extracurricular activities and family dinners. He recalls fondly the home cooked meals every night and the family discussions around the dinner table.

An emerging pattern that Daniel began to reveal was one of perfectionism and performance. The image of the family was treated as more important than identifying conflicting issues, that when confronted, usually help family members to grow. Daniel identified, after revealing his history that he never wanted to be seen as a disappointment to his parents.

EXERCISE:

History

The following questions will help build your awareness of historical feeling states or experiences that may seem like normal events to you but may still be trigger points. You may also have significant recollection of events but you may not have an awareness of the body memories and the visceral counterparts of these memories. Some events may have been processed and laid to rest and you may not have considered them in this context. However, revealing your history thoroughly is paramount to resolving the phenomenon of Vicarious Trauma.

As you move through the exercises below, be patient. Go slowly and become introspective in a gentle and self-accepting manner. The purpose of revealing your history is not to judge or evaluate; it is simply to honor and acknowledge.

YOUR PARENTS, YOUR FAMILY AND YOUR WORDLY ATTACHMENTS

Describe your early memories of your mother with five adjectives:

1. _____

2. _____

3. _____

4. _____

5. _____

Describe your early memories of your father with five adjectives:

1. _____

2. _____

3. _____

4. _____

5. _____

Did your family suffer a life altering event such as a death or divorce? If so, how was this addressed by your immediate family?_____

_____

_____

_____

_____

If you lived in a blended family system, please describe the dynamics associated with this experience. _____

_____

_____

_____

_____

Imagine watching an old movie of yourself as a child. Describe what you see._____

_____

_____

_____

_____

Describe your parents' marriage with five adjectives:

1. _____

2. _____

3. _____

4. _____

5. _____

How did your parents/step-parents resolve their conflicts? What did you see? What did you hear or not hear? _____

_____

_____

_____

_____

How did you feel when your parents/step-parents were having conflicts? _____

_____

_____

_____

_____

How did you feel when conflicts went unaddressed by your family? _____

_____

_____

_____

_____

How did your parents/step-parents handle issues around money?_____

_____

_____

_____

_____

How did your parents/step-parents handle issues around religion? _____

_____

_____

_____

_____

How did your parents/step-parents handle issues around food?_____

_____

_____

_____

_____

How did your family have fun together? _____

_____

_____

_____

_____

How was affection displayed in your family? _____

_____

_____

_____

_____

How were issues around sex approached in your family?_____

_____

_____

_____

_____

How was illness addressed in your family? _____

_____

_____

_____

_____

_____

Was there any addiction or substance abuse in your family? If so, how did it you affect you?_____

_____

_____

_____

_____

What was the role of extended family? _____

_____

_____

_____

_____

How were you disciplined? _____

_____

_____

_____

_____

How were your relationships with your siblings? What was your birth order? _____

_____

_____

_____

_____

What are your most vivid memories? _____

_____

_____

_____

_____

What were your greatest joys as a child? _____

_____

_____

_____

_____

What scared you as a child? _____

_____

_____

_____

_____

What were some ways you used to distract yourself
when you felt afraid or upset? Some examples might be
daydreaming, thumb sucking, nail biting, masturbating,
nightmares, bed wetting, temper tantrums, withdrawal,
bullying, underachieving, over-achieving, lying or crying. _

_____

_____

_____

_____

_____

How did you get attention? _____

_____

_____

_____

_____

Some Common Childhood Fears

A dark closet

Being accosted by a scary child

Being caught in the rain

Coming home to an empty house

Hearing strange noises

Having nightmares

Losing a friend

Losing a love

Accidents

Public embarrassment

Surgery

Illness

Moving

Missing out on important events

Hospital Stays

Shyness

Did you have any behavioral problems as a child? _____

_____

_____

_____

_____

Did you have any particular challenges in growing up that stand out in your memory such as poverty, illness, learning disabilities, disappointments, deaths, divorce, etc?

_____

_____

_____

_____

_____

YOUR EDUCATIONAL EXPERIENCES:

Describe your experience in elementary school. _____

_____

_____

_____

_____

Describe your experience in middle school. _____

_____

_____

_____

_____

Describe your experience in high school. _____

_____

_____

_____

_____

Did you change schools while you were growing up? If so, how often? _____

_____

_____

_____

_____

If you moved, how did it affect your relationships? _____

_____

_____

_____

_____

How did your parents explain the moves?_____

_____

_____

_____

_____

How did your family communicate about important life changes?_____

_____

_____

_____

_____

Describe any other significant relationships that you had while growing up: friendships, romances, relationships with grandparents, aunts, uncles, teachers or other authority figures, peer groups, extracurricular activities you participated in, etc. _____

_____

_____

_____

_____

_____

EXERCISE:

What patterns do you see emerging as you reveal certain aspects of your history? How you developed and evolved is important to how you cope today. Our goal here is that become identifiable to you. Examples of patterns that you may acknowledge are Avoidant, Passive, Aggressive, Passive-Aggressive, Abusive, Neglectful, Overprotective, Depressed, Anxious, Disconnected, Numb, Silent, Addictive, Oppositional, Bystanding, Perfectionism, etc. You may come up with a pattern of your own that is not mentioned here. No one knows your history better than you do!

Historical Patterns of Coping
Avoidant
Passive
Aggressive
Passive-Aggressive
Abusive
Neglectful
Overprotective
Depressed
Anxious
Disconnected
Numb
Silent
Addictive
Oppositional
Bystanding
Perfectionism

_____

_____

_____

_____

_____

_____

_____

_____

_____

EXERCISE:

Judgments and Evaluations

After revealing your history, identify and write down some judgments and evaluations you began to make about yourself and your place in the world as you moved through the early developmental stages of life. For example, a child who had a chronically ill mother may have perceived themselves as abandoned and alone, as a caretaker for that parent, or as a surrogate partner for the other parent. Another example is adopted children may have frequently felt sad because they perceived themselves as outsiders or in a state of perpetual disconnect. A child of addictive parents may have judged themselves as unworthy of attention and regard because the addictive substance took over the family system. A child of divorce may have judged themselves as the cause and therefore, not lovable enough to keep the family intact. These types of self-judgments, while untrue, are natural conclusions for a child to draw because at an early stage of development, children are egocentric and tend to perceive themselves as the center of the universe. As adults, it is our wish for you to begin to identify and address these faulty core beliefs.

Write down the judgments you made about yourself as a child growing up in the context of your family._____

_____

_____

_____

_____

_____

_____

_____

_____

_____

_____

_____

STEP TWO

Recognizing Your Impasse

IT IS

History repeats itself. Even history that we don't recall repeats itself. Revealing your history is an empowering first step. Now we would like you to consider how you might unwittingly re-create some early patterns in your current life that you have already identified in the preceding chapter.

Those who have unconscious or unresolved fears and judgments about themselves are at risk of repeating the pattern in their primary relationships, in their parenting and in their work. They are also at the greatest risk for suffering unidentified Vicarious Trauma.

The Impasse is defined as an emotional and physiological fear reaction; that point of a fear reaction that has its roots in our history. This reaction has three dimensions: 1) the memory itself, 2) the negative feeling you have attached to it, and, 3) the judgment we make of ourselves and the others involved in it. When triggered, we continue to distract ourselves, believing that it is a form of self-protection, when in reality the only thing that is being protected is the historical fear itself. The unconscious purpose of defending your Impasse is to protect yourself from ever having to feel the fear that originated in early childhood. Children normally find ways to distract themselves from feeling afraid simply because fear is an overwhelming feeling state. A child does not yet possess the skills or the internal tools to manage fear.

As adults, rather than resort to distraction from the fear, we need to recognize it, turn into it, and overcome it. Until now, we have used various distractions to avoid the unpleasant feeling state. Distraction is historically based, and we deserve and need to recognize the distraction we are unconsciously using to cover the original fear that drove the historically based distraction. We are now ready to move into the fear and not into the distraction. Let us recognize the originating fear and identify it. We will call this the Impasse. Here is Daniel's experience with this step.

Daniel: Recognizing the Impasse

Our job now was to help Daniel discover, in what was a seemingly innocuous family history, the emotional impasse that was becoming triggered for him through this particular case. When the client in question came to retain Daniel, and proceeded to talk about the alleged sexual impropriety, Daniel noticed himself feeling agitated and anxious. He would come to understand that he was at an impasse and he was compromised in his ability to remain professionally present.

When asked to recall an event in growing up that really stood out for him, he paused and then began to share with us a rather enlightening historical event. When he was six years old, he and a group of neighborhood children were playing in a neighbor's garage. They were playing doctor, examining each other and looking at the differences in their anatomy. The little girls were fascinated with the fact that he had a penis and he was fascinated with their vaginas. They played for a while and then all went home, except for him and a friend, who went to play at the friend's home. After what he recalls as about an hour, his mother called and requested that he come home immediately. Daniel left and walked home.

When he arrived, his mother and father were in the kitchen, and asked him if he had taken his pants off with the other neighborhood children. He immediately sensed that his parents were angry and he didn't understand why. He innocently agreed that he did, in fact, do that and Lori, a little girl, showed him her private parts, and that he showed her his private parts.

His mother became enraged and told him to drop his pants. She was going to spank him for his behavior. She screamed at him, telling him that he embarrassed her and his Dad with Lori's parents and all the other parents in the neighborhood. They contended that he did something terribly wrong and that he should never ever do it again.

He was spanked with a wooden spoon by his mother until he screamed at her to stop. During this act of corporal punishment, his father sat in the other room, silent. The subject was never again brought up in the family, as if it never happened. At this point, Daniel stated, "Wow! That's really a disturbing memory. I haven't thought of that in over 25 years". He recognized that this self-described distressing event had in fact deeply affected him. As a result of the case he was presently working on, Daniel realized that this event or impasse carried a lot more significance for him than he was ever conscious about.

Daniel then told us that he had many friendships and relationships as his childhood progressed, but always felt uncomfortable about his body and about his sexual ability. Later, in his junior year of high school, he became serious about a girl and they began having a sexual relationship. One evening, about six months into the relationship, his girlfriend's father called his mother to let her know that Daniel was having sexual relations with their daughter and that they (her parents) were upset. Daniel's mother spoke with him about this conversation and directed him to discontinue his relationship with this young woman. She maintained that risking his future on a girl at this point might ruin his chances for college and law school. He related that several days later, in silent resentment and grief, he broke up with his girlfriend. He did this to avoid disappointing his mother and to avoid a conflict. He could now see that this was one of numerous other times he had unwittingly re-created his original impasse.

After Daniel told us his story, we asked him if he felt these incidents broke his spirit. His facial expression visibly softened and he sank back into his chair. He said, "You're so right. I never thought of it that way," and he began to weep.

The self-protective distractions of our childhood mature as we develop. Now that you have revealed your history, you are able to become conscious about and recognize how you find yourself at your own Impasse repeatedly in adulthood and even more so through your work as a *helper*.

EXERCISE:

Childhood Distractions and Coping Mechanisms

Let us recognize how this applies to you. Think again and repeat the identification of childhood distractions/coping mechanisms you utilized when you felt afraid. List them below. _____

_____

_____

_____

_____

_____

EXERCISE:

Evolved Distractions

Now contemplate the more adult behaviors that you do today that might be considered "evolved distractions" of your childhood reactions to fear. For example, a thumb-sucker or a nail biter may now be a cigarette smoker; a shy child may be a socially withdrawn adult; a child that used illness for attention may be chronically ill as an adult; an over-achiever may turn into a workaholic; a bully might grow up to struggle with road rage. List the adult distractions you use below._____

_____

_____

_____

_____

_____

_____

_____

When you peel away the distractions, you might notice that you are experiencing anxiety. Underlying historical fear is an internally divisive dynamic, a primitive, limbic brain neurocircuitry that inhibits individuals from accessing their higher thinking. As a child, you hadn't yet fully formed your pre-frontal cortex. This area of the brain embodies the higher mind and the behavioral responses of courage, trust and faith in one's ability to overcome fear. (See Chapter 3, The Neuroscience of Trauma, Second-Hand Shock: Surviving & Overcoming Vicarious Trauma, 2010). The anxiety people feel when they stop distracting themselves is a form of separation anxiety, emptiness or void resulting from being in disconnect from the higher mind.

As an adult this part of your brain has developed and needs to be more regularly accessed as a healthy coping mechanism for dealing with trauma. Training our brains to move into this higher functioning is derailed when we continue to distract it with childhood coping mechanisms rather than adult responses. Our goal is to mend the spiritual bridge or neural pathways to your spiritual mind and that part of your higher brain.

EXERCISE:

Journaling

a. It is now time to think about and write down some client stories you have felt particularly uncomfortable with or that evoked a body reaction- like anger, or anxiety- after listening to the content. Use your journal for this exercise.

b. Recognize when you are playing an updated version of an historical scene and allow yourself to experience rather than avoid the unpleasant separation anxiety that gets triggered in the replay. You need to experience your legitimate anxiety in order to heal.

c. Now write in your journal a personal historical story that comes to mind for you by virtue of having listened to the client's story.

After you have finished journaling, say to yourself, "Something is getting triggered in me. This is not about the client. This is about what the client's story is activating in my own historical neurocircuitry. It's okay that this is going on for me. I will not judge it. I will remain calm so that I may identify what is coming to the surface. By identifying and getting conscious of it, I will better serve my client. Also, I don't have to react the way I did as a child. I am an adult now and have other choices. I do not have to distract myself from this upset in order to prevail. Instead, I need to feel it, move through it, and remember that my incident was in the past and does not have to hold any meaning for me in the present. It is powerless over me today."

d. Write down in your journal the subjects that trigger your impasses: (Some examples might be childhood violence, molestation, abandonment, corporal punishment, divorce, death of a family member, death of a child, moving, an angry father/mother, a passive mother/father, peer rejection, failure at something you attempted, bullying, cheating, accidents, foul weather, illness, addictions, neglect, certain words, the parental "look", etc.)

e. Put your Impasse into words in your journal. Remember, your Impasse contains your memory of the event, your feeling about the event when it happened and how you judged yourself or others involved in light of the event.

No one knows your Impasse better than you. Develop an inner of awareness of your Impasse and make friends with it. Don't avoid it any more. Right now we ask you to recognize it so you can move forward and think peacefully about it.

STEP THREE

Release Your Past

I CAN

Your unconscious attachment to some parts of your past prohibit you from bridging to the higher mind or spiritual self, which is the most powerful and peaceful part of you. The spiritual self stays peacefully centered in the here and now. Having identified your Impasse and deciding no longer to retreat from it, you can begin to mend the break in your spiritual bridge. It is important to note that this break widens in your work with trauma content. By releasing the past, you can exchange your purpose from protecting an historical fear to healing your connection to hope and peacefulness. You are now beginning to form more remedial neural pathways that will empower you to negotiate trauma material more resourcefully.

In releasing the past you must remember that your memories don't equal the past. What you remember has far less impact than how you remember it. The historical action itself is over. It is only your judgment of yourself and others in its context that remains. For example, if you have a memory of being disciplined by an aggressive parent, there may be a childlike part of you that remembers this event with embarrassment or shame, believing in some way you were not worthy of receiving love. The memory itself is far less damaging than your perception of who you are in light of it. If you are working with a client who is grieving about abuse they suffered at the heavy hand of a parent or spouse, you yourself may go into a shame spiral due to the triggering of your own childhood impasses.

You can heal your perception of a painful historical event anytime you choose to relinquish judgment of that event. Let's witness how Daniel addressed his own historical judgments.

Daniel: Releasing The Past

As Daniel acknowledged and honored his Impasse he realized that the boy who was spanked perceived himself as dirty, inappropriate and not deserving of being loved. His memory of playing doctor with the neighborhood children was not as troublesome as his judgment of himself around it, which was that he was an inappropriate child who deserved to be punished. How sad for little Daniel, we pointed out, for he was only having normal childhood curiosity about human anatomy.

Daniel worked to release his past by relinquishing judgment around the spanking. He realized for the first time that much of the shame he carried actually belonged to his mother, who herself was embarrassed within her community by her son's participation in playing doctor. Her son should have known better.

As a young boy in that event, Daniel judged his mother as perpetrating, attacking, rejecting and angry. He judged his father as abandoning, powerless and absent. As an adult, Daniel has the choice to no longer attribute these judgments to himself, his mother or his father. He exchanged his purpose from fear to forgiveness and in so doing, released his painful perception of that aspect of his past.

EXERCISE:

Impasse Memories

a. Review and write down the historical events that you identified as Impasses. _____

_____

_____

_____

b. Correlate and write down the feelings you had with those particular Impasse memories. Painful memories might typically elicit feeling states of sadness, embarrassment, shame, disappointment, anger or fear. These feelings, untreated, may generate a personal and professional sense of inadequacy. (Daniel put the following feelings around his Impasse: shame, sadness, anger, and most of all, fear of disappointing his parents.)

> *Painful memories might typically elicit feeling states of:*
>
> Sadness
> Embarrassment
> Shame
> Disappointment
> Anger
> Fear

c. List the judgments you've made about yourself or others around these Impasse events. _____

_____

_____

_____

_____

EXERCISE:

Exchanging Fear for Forgiveness

In order to relinquish the judgment, you now need to exchange your fear for forgiveness.

a. Admit you have the fear. Write down what you are afraid of (e.g., I have a fear of not being good enough, of being stupid, embarrassed, etc.)_____

_____

_____

_____

_____

b. Take personal responsibility for the role your memory is playing in your life and decide what it is you want to create around this memory (e.g., healing, peace, calmness, closure, release or forgiveness versus resentment, anger, hostility, grievance, continued pain, vengeance, depression, anxiety or physical illness). Write it down. _____

_____

_____

_____

_____

c. Realize the judgment you have placed on the event and on the person or persons in the event with you. List these judgments. _____

_____

_____

_____

_____

d. Remove all descriptors (adjectives or adverbs) that depict this event.

Daniel addressed this by writing in his journal:

> *"I was playing doctor with my friends and we were curious about each other's bodies and examined each other. We were different, as some of us were girls and some were boys. I took my pants off and the girl next door took her pants off. We giggled because I had a penis and she didn't. That was it, nothing more. We pulled up our pants and went out to play. Later that night my mother asked me if I took off my clothes at Lori's house. I said yes. She hit me with a wooden spoon on my bare bottom until I cried. It just was. It's not happening now and I don't need to feel anything about it at all. I certainly don't need to be afraid. If my mother came at me with a wooden spoon today, I could protect myself and stop her. As a child, I had no recourse. My parents' past disapproval doesn't mean I am a bad child. I am choosing to release this feeling of unworthiness because I can."*

e. Remove all your judgments, unconsciously made at an earlier time, from the description of the event. Commit to exchanging your fear around this event with forgiveness; forgiveness of yourself and forgiveness of the others who were involved. <u>You do not have to forgive the event itself. The event may not have been okay.</u> You are forgiving yourself and the other people involved so you can be released. Remember, this forgiveness is not for them – it is for **you** to be free. It is through your forgiveness of the other person that you can be released from a painful past.

f. Write in your journal, I forgive...........(e.g. my mother for hitting me with a wooden spoon, and I forgive myself for..................(e.g. any negative self judgments I have made in light of or because of this event).

Forgiveness is for people, not for actions. Spanking is an action; because you were spanked doesn't mean you were bad. Maybe you engaged in behavior that was unacceptable; that doesn't mean you are unacceptable. You made a mistake, you are not a mistake.

EXERCISE:

Personal Obstacles

What are your personal obstacles to forgiveness (for example, some people see themselves as justified in bearing grievances)?

In deciding to release the past, you can move from fear to forgiveness. Forgiveness is the relinquishment of judgment followed by a thought of peace. You can now remember that in light of a painful memory, you remain worthy of compassion and regard. The thoughts of peace will now serve us in your next step: ***responding* to fear.**

STEP FOUR

Respond To Your Fear
I KNOW

There is a big difference between *responding* and *reacting*. Reacting involves little or no spiritual connection. It is based on the limbic brain's instinct of fight, flight or freeze and is defensive in nature. We react when we perceive the need to protect ourselves. If we take ourselves back to the first step, we are invested in protecting ourselves from feeling historical fears. To do so is faulty thinking and a dangerous place to put oneself in the *helping* relationship.

Responding involves the introduction of a reply or an answer and is associated with the conscious left brain. Take a second and consider how you tend to answer in emotionally charged or fearful conditions. Daniel, the family lawyer in our case study, would become a perfectionist and a workaholic when he felt afraid.

Once we have relinquished our earlier self-judgment unconsciously that was unconsciously made, we need to stay peaceful when we are presented with an upsetting work situation that triggers fear from our limbic brain. *Responding*, rather than *reacting*, implies thinking peacefully or calmly when we are deciding what to do or what to say in a fear-provoking situation. *Responding* rather than *reacting* to emotional fear is the most important part of recovering from Vicarious Trauma. *Responding* is a discipline. It requires a great deal of mental structure and practice in order to become proficient at it.

Now that you have revealed your history, recognized your impasse and made a commitment to release the past, you are ready to respond to the historical fear that gets triggered through your personal relationships and your work.

EXERCISE:

Stop, Look and Listen

Do you remember this phrase being taught to you as a child when you were learning to cross the street? Some streets are easier to cross than others. At some of the dangerous intersections, you could easily be mowed down by a vehicle if you didn't adhere to the rule. When you find yourself at a scary emotional intersection in your work, the rule of *responding* is to stop, look and listen.

Stop: identify what will become your personal red light. What was once a burden in your distraction from fear can now serve as a blessing in that it signals something is being triggered for you. Simply stop. What is your adult distraction when you feel afraid? Here are some possibilities: raging, numbing out, drinking, drugs, withdrawing, isolating, stealing, shopping, dissociating, impatience, passivity, eating disorders, working too much, headaches, stomach aches, ringing in the ears, intrusive thoughts, nightmares, sleeping, fuzzy thinking, or forgetting to breathe. What are yours? Keep in mind that it could be more than one symptom.

Look: look inside and become introspective and think about what is being triggered in your history? Acknowledge it. Honor it. Relinquish judgment about yourself and others involved. Think peacefully about it. Forgive it. For example, if your paternal abandonment is being triggered by a client's story, and you have stopped the distracting behaviors you used to engage in, you have now freed yourself to look inward and reveal your truth as to what is happening.

Listen: Listen to your inner voice and your inner truth.

EXERCISE:

Journaling

a. Go to your journal and write about a time when a particular client story triggered something personal for you. As you write it, you can listen peacefully to your inner story and realize you deserve to forgive, to be forgiven and to be more patient with yourself and the traumatizing aspects of your work.

b. Write your story so that the concluding line is "May this story rest in peace".

Practice the two forgiveness steps:

1) relinquishing judgment, followed by

2) thoughts of peace.

c. In the space below, make a forgiveness list for hurts you have incurred in your personal life and in the workplace. Every story is an opportunity for practicing forgiveness which has been coined for centuries as being divine. _____

_____
_____
_____
_____
_____

d. Make a list of all the people you want to forgive and include the things you believe you need to be forgiven. _____

_____
_____
_____
_____
_____

This practice is universally healing and the person doing the forgiving is successfully bridging to his/her higher mind, creating new found hope, faith and meaning in his/her life and ultimately, in his/ her work. Let's have a look at how our client Daniel responded to fear.

Daniel: Responding to Fear

As he recognized the Impasse and relinquished the self-judgment, Daniel was now conscious when the historical fear of being unworthy and a disappointment was triggered in his work and in his family. He could now respond to this fear rather than distract himself from it by working harder, obsessing about a particular case or becoming physically ill. He began to practice thinking peacefully about that painful childhood event, forgiving his parents and himself. He was able to notice more frequently when he was triggered in his work. When he became a perfectionist, he stopped, looked within and listened to his inner story. Instead of being traumatized vicariously, he remembered what was really going on for him and responded to the fear with kindness and peace unto himself. By doing this repeatedly, he began to mend the break in his spiritual bridge and develop an improved neural pathway to his higher brain, which he could now more easily access.

STEP FIVE

Reconnect To Your Spirit

I AM

This is the most rewarding part of the process. There is nothing you have to do. There is nothing you have to figure out. Simply let your mind be still. Now that you are no longer distracted, anxious, worried or fearful, you have opened the way to clear your mind and allow your neurons to bridge to your higher thinking where you receive the gifts of your spiritual perspective.

Now that you are no longer distracted and can let your mind be still, you are empowered to start engaging in some practice that will allow wisdom, calm and peaceful thoughts into your experience. Let your mind receive and connect to them. Develop a spirituality/peace plan, something that you will do daily, weekly, monthly to clear your mind and allow the spiritual traits to come into your thinking.

Peace Plan Possibilities:		
Meditation	Speaking your truth	Exercising
Prayer	Engaging in the arts	Joining an encouragement group
Nature hikes	Reading	
Gardening	Journaling	Dancing,
12-step programs	Playing games	Cooking
Connecting with others	Expressing gratitude	Sports

EXERCISE:

Wish List

Write down all the things that you wish you had the time to do and haven't been able to fit into your schedule._____

_____

_____

EXERCISE:

Modifying your Schedule:

Look at your schedule and see how you can modify it so that your personal spirit has time to rejuvenate. Put in blocks of time throughout your schedule to release the pressures and stresses of the day and see where you can fit in some of the things you have wanted to do but have not prioritized.

EXERCISE:

Affirmations

Make 5 affirmations that you can repeat – one for each day of the work week. For example:

- I am going to face my week with courage, tolerance and patience.

- My work is busy and meaningful. I am grateful for the help I can give.

- I will be introspective today. I will think of any upsetting situations that have occurred so far and address them with the Process I have learned.

- Today I will nurture myself- the work week is drawing to a close and I will plan some self-fulfilling activities in the two or three days ahead.

- I have completed a challenging week. There have been satisfying and taxing experiences. I have helped others and learned some important things about myself.

- I have stayed in the present and not allowed my past to dictate how I lead my life today.

- I have not been distracted with inappropriate behaviors.

- I am proud of my recovery from Vicarious Trauma and will continue to work on it every day.

Now, write your own.

1. _____

2. _____

3. _____

4. _____

5. _____

Commit to follow through with your plan.

Here is a final look at Daniel as he reconnected to his higher mind.

Daniel: Reconnecting to the Spirit

Daniel saw us for five sessions. During the fifth session he reported that since he was thinking more peacefully, he noticed a renewed ability to utilize abstract spiritual behaviors such as hope, courage and faith in himself. He relaxed more around his cases, set clearer boundaries in his work life and spent more time with his family. As Daniel became more conscious of remembering his spiritual connection, he was able to pick and choose from his own religious historical practices he could draw upon, add to and share with his family. He terminated his treatment with us feeling a rich gratitude for all the wonderful things in his life: his own personal well-being, a loving wife, great kids and a rewarding career.

This is a creative journey. You will decide how to build a spiritual perspective that fits into your lifestyle and belief system. Any combination of behaviors that fit for you will work – it's a very personal creation. Communing with nature, sitting in a sauna, relaxing in a hammock, reading a book, spending time with loved ones, gardening, cooking, singing, getting a massage, exercising; whatever brings you joy. It doesn't have to be religious in nature although it could be or it could be a patchwork design representing a number of gratifying activities. Whatever resonates for you, we wish you peace.

CHAPTER 4

Conclusion

Spread the Word!

It is our hope that completing this workbook has given you appreciation and new found sensitivity to the stressors of your work. We hope this has struck a chord in you that will allow you to become passionate about the reality of Vicarious Trauma and spread the word in your *helping* circles and around your community in general. We encourage you to consider starting Vicarious Trauma support groups, and/or staff meetings where traumatizing interactions can be debriefed and resolved.

We aspire to raise the social consciousness about the prevalence and seriousness of Vicarious Trauma so that our heroes will be treated as precious human beings with feelings and struggles of their own. Social acknowledgement, treatment centers, recuperative programs and retreats should be commonplace and highly available to professionals who function as helpers. We need your help in this endeavor.

CONTACT INFORMATION

Ellie and Vicki serve as directors of the Vicarious Trauma Institute in Scottsdale, Arizona. They can be contacted at (480) 991-4119, or by email at:

ellieizzo@vicarioustrauma.com

or

vcarpelmiller@vicarioustrauma.com

The Vicarious Trauma Institute, based in Scottsdale, Arizona, serves clients from any and all helping professions, providing individual consultations, 1- 3-day intensive treatment programs, and recuperative retreats. We support you in searching out any professional who is knowledgeable in this field and encourage you to utilize any resources that help address your Vicarious Trauma. We look forward to working with you.

Ellie and Vicki
www.vicarioustrauma.com

BIBLIOGRAPHY

Begley, S. (2007). *Train Your Mind, Change Your Brain.* NY: Ballantine.

Carll, E. (2006). Trauma psychology: the evolution of a specialty; *APA.* Online. Google. 28 Feb. 2007. [http://www.division42.org].

Earley, J. (2006). Countertransference patterns. *Transference and Countertransference.* Online. Google, 8 June 2007. [http://www.earley.org./Patterns/Transference_and_countertransference].

Figley, C.R.. (Ed.) (1995). *Compassion fatigue: Coping with secondary traumatic stress disorder in those who treat the traumatized.* NY: Brunner Mazel.

Fox, R. & Carey, L. (1999). Therapists' collusion with the resistance of rape survivors. *Clinical Social Work Journal.* Summer 185-201.

Frankl, Victor. (19540. *Man's Search for meaning: An introduction to logotherapy.* NY: Washington Square Press.

International Trauma Consultants. (2006). Online. Google. 6 Mar. 2007. [http://www.traumaconsultants.net].

Jaffe, J., Segal, J., Dumke, l. (2005). Emotional and psychological trauma. Online. Google. 2 Feb. 2007. [http://www.helpguide.org].

Joseph, R. (1999). The neurology of traumatic 'dissociative' amnesia: commentary & literature review. *Child Abuse and Neglect.* Aug. 23(8). 715-727.

Kramer, P.(2007). Empathy. *The Infinite Mind.* Online. Google. [http://www.kmedia.com].

Kennedy, E. & Charles, S. On Becoming a Counselor: A Basic Guide for Non-professional Counselors. NY: Crossroads.

Lee, Daniel. (2006). The hidden costs of trauma in the workplace. Online. Google. 6 March 2007. [http://www.humannatureatwork.com/workplacestress.

Liberzon, I., Taylor, S., Amdur, R., Jung, T., Chamberlin, K, Minoshima, S., Koeppe, R., & Fig, L. (1999). Brain activation in POST TRAUMATIC STRESS DISORDER in response to trauma related stimuli. *Biological Psychiatry*. 45(7). 817-826.

Pearlman, L. & Mac Ian, P. (1995). An empirical study of the effects of trauma on work with trauma therapists. *Professional Psychology: Research and Practice*. 26(6). 558-565.

Pearlman, L., Saakvitne, K. Figley, C. (1995). Treating therapists and vicarious traumatization and secondary traumatic stress disorders in *Treating Compassion Fatigue*. NY: Brunner Mazel. 150-177.

Saakvitne, K. & Pearlman, L. (1996). *Transforming the Pain: a Workbook on Vicarious Trauma*. NY: W.W. Norton.

Schore, A. (2003). Advances in neuropsychoanalysis attachment theory and trauma research. *Psychoanalytic Inquiry*. 22. 433-484.

Stamm, B. H. (Ed.) (1995) *Secondary traumatic stress: Self-care issues for clinician, researchers and educators*. Lutherville, MD: Sidran.

Weingarten, K. (2004). Common shock: witnessing violence in clients' lives (adaptation). *Counselor Magazine*. Feb. 2004. 70-74.

Weingarten, K. (2003). *Common Shock: Witnessing Violence Every Day: How We are Harmed, How We can Heal*. NY: Dutton.

Wilson, J. & Lindy, J. (1994). *Countertransference in the Treatment of POST TRAUMATIC STRESS DISORDER*. NY: Guilford Press.

Wilson, J. & Thomas, R. (2004). *Empathy and the Treatment of Trauma and POST TRAUMATIC STRESS DISORDER*. NY: Brunner Mazel.

REFERENCES

Baldwin, D. (2007). About Trauma. Online. Google. 28 May 2007.
[http://www.trauma_pages.com/trauma].

Begley, S. (2007). *Train Your Mind, Change Your Brain*. NY: Ballantine.

Berne, Eric (1964). *The Games People Play*. NY: Ballantine.

Carll, E. (2006). Trauma psychology: the evolution of a specialty; *APA*. Online.
Google. 28 Feb. 2007. [http://www.division42.org].

Earley, J. (2006). Countertransference patterns. *Transference and Countertransference*.
Online. Google, 8 June 2007.
[http://www.earley.org./Patterns/Transference_and_countertransference].

Fox, R. & Carey, L. (1999). Therapists' collusion with the resistance of rape survivors.
Clinical Social Work Journal. Summer 185-201.

Healing Resources Info. (2005) *Santa Barbara Graduate Institute for Clinical Studies and
Research*. Online. Google. 28 May 2004. [http://www.traumaresources.org].

International Trauma Consultants. (2006). Online. Google. 6 Mar. 2007.
[http://www.traumaconsultants.net].

Jaffe, J., Segal, J., Dumke, l. (2005). Emotional and psychological trauma. Online.
Google. 2 Feb. 2007. [http://www.helpguide.org].

Joseph, R. (1999). The neurology of traumatic 'dissociative' amnesia: commentary &
literature review. *Child Abuse and Neglect*. Aug. 23(8). 715-727.

Kramer, P.(2007). Empathy. *The Infinite Mind*. Online. Google.
[http://www.kmedia.com].

Kennedy, E. & Charles, S. On Becoming a Counselor: *A Basic Guide for Non-professional Counselors.* NY: Crossroads.

Lee, Daniel. (2006). The hidden costs of trauma in the workplace. Online. Google. 6 March 2007. [http://www.humannatureatwork.com/workplacestress].

Liberzon, I., Taylor, S., Amdur, R., Jung, T., Chamberlin, K, Minoshima, S., Koeppe, R., & Fig, L. (1999). Brain activation in POST TRAUMATIC STRESS DISORDER in response to trauma related stimuli. *Biological Psychiatry.* 45(7). 817-826.

McSwain, K., Robinson, R., Panteluk, L. (1998). Implications for practice: therapeutic, personal and organizational coping strategies. *Second Annual Poster Session.* Online. Google. 28 may 2007. [http://www.dr.jontry.com].

Pearlman, L. & Mac Ian, P. (1995). An empirical study of the effects of trauma on work with trauma therapists. *Professional Psychology: Research and Practice.* 26(6). 558-565.

Pearlman, L., Saakvitne, K. Figley, C. (1995). Treating therapists and vicarious traumatization and secondary traumatic stress disorders in *Treating Compassion Fatigue.* NY: Brunner Mazel. 150-177.

Saakvitne, K. & Pearlman, L. (1996). *Transforming the Pain: a Workbook on Vicarious Trauma.* NY: W.W. Norton.

Santy, P. (2007) Feeling, countertransference, and reality. Online. Google. 8 June 2007. [http://www.blog.spot.com/2006].

Schore, A. (2003). Advances in neuropsychoanalysis attachment theory and trauma research. *Psychoanalytic Inquiry.* 22. 433-484.

Weingarten, K. (2004). Common shock: witnessing violence in clients' lives (adaptation). *Counselor Magazine.* Feb. 2004. 70-74.

Weingarten, K. (2003). *Common Shock: Witnessing Violence Every Day: How We are Harmed, How We can Heal.* NY: Dutton.

Wilson, J. & Lindy, J. (1994). *Countertransference in the Treatment of Post Traumatic Stress Disorder.* NY: Guilford Press.

Wilson, J. & Thomas, R. (2004). *Empathy and the Treatment of Trauma and Post Traumatic Stress Disorder.* NY: Brunner Mazel.

CPSIA information can be obtained at www.ICGtesting.com
Printed in the USA
BVOW011557180413

318466BV00007B/21/P